Feature Writing for Newspapers

FEATURE WRITING FOR NEWSPAPERS

by DANIEL R. WILLIAMSON

COMMUNICATION ARTS BOOKS

HASTINGS HOUSE, PUBLISHERS

New York 10016

Library of Congress Cataloging in Publication Data

Williamson, Daniel Raymond, 1943-
  Feature writing for newspapers.

  Communication arts books)
  Includes index.
  1. Journalism—Authorship. I. Title.

PN4775.W63   808'.066'07019   75-17898
ISBN 0-8038-2312-6
ISBN 0-8038-2313-4 pbk.

Published simultaneously in Canada by
Saunders of Toronto, Ltd., Don Mills, Ontario

Designed by Al Lichtenberg
Printed in the United States of America

Contents

Preface

Writing a journalism textbook is a complicated project because of the peculiar nature of the profession.

While physical sciences deal in formulas and rules that are unvarying and predictable, journalism deals in the most unpredictable and mercurial subject of all: human nature. Because of this unstable commodity, any attempt at teaching journalistic writing through a series of absolute, unvarying rules or formulas is patently absurd.

Instead, the journalism teacher must confine his efforts to those of *defining* the basic elements of the trade and explaining the many techniques which have evolved not from a controlled, laboratory situation, but from years of trial and error. Many techniques are passed on from one generation of reporters to another through word of mouth —not by textbook.

In *Feature Writing for Newspapers*, the author has explained the various techniques and lessons within the context of actual newspaper experiences. Examples used in this text are based on the author's own experiences as a reporter for *The Daily News* of Dayton, Ohio, or upon the experiences of his former colleagues.

Besides adding clarity, the technique of relating lessons to the experiences enables the student to "witness" the complete production of many types of stories, from the moment that the idea is conceived to the final period of the finished copy. Hopefully, this technique will not only give readers a "feel" for reporting, but it will enhance the readability of the text.

Although all the essentials in feature writing are presented, prospective journalists should be forewarned that the textbook is not a do-it-yourself guide to a Pulitzer Prize. Writing is an art that requires great dedication, discipline and practice. Talent and technical knowledge are useless without a large share of the other virtues listed.

A good journalist is an idealist, where his profession is concerned. He doesn't write to please himself. He is dedicated to serving the readers who trust him to provide accurate and complete information, upon which they may exercise their democratic prerogatives. Often, he will work many hours without extra pay or reward to do the best possible job. This kind of dedication cannot be taught in book form.

In writing this textbook, the author discovered that he is indebted to many people who, to varying degrees, contributed to his professional knowledge:

From the University of Alabama Department of Journalism: Professors Charles Scarritt (retired), John Luskin (retired), and Miriam Hill, who taught the author the "basics" of journalism.

From The Birmingham News, Jerry Proctor, who provided on-the-job training for the application of those techniques.

From The Daily News in Dayton, Ohio: Managing Editor Arnold Rosenfeld, who gave permission for reprinting stories from The Daily News, City Editor James Dygert, and newsmen Randy Preddy, Dave Herd, Gene Goltz, Dale Huffman, and many others, who by word or by example contributed techniques and principles that are included.

From The University of Northern Colorado: Dr. William Hartman, Chairman of the Department of Journalism, who gave much needed encouragement to the project; and to UNC Journalism students who inspired—demanded—the lectures from which this textbook grew.

Finally, the author wishes to especially acknowledge the contribution of his children, John and Barbara, who donated their father's time to this project.

Most of all, the author acknowledges the encouragement and patience of his wife, Diane, by dedicating this book to her.

DANIEL R. WILLIAMSON

1 What Is Feature Writing?

You are a general assignment reporter for the Capitol City *News*. While driving home from work, you pass over a drawbridge and see a solitary man inside a small shelter. You've passed over the bridge hundreds of times before without a second thought, but suddenly, you pull to the curb and grab your notepad. You have just spotted a feature story.

A half hour later, you emerge from the shelter with several pages of notes, after interviewing John Dalton, the drawbridge operator. Dalton's job is to raise the bridge whenever a large riverboat approaches. Only three or four large riverboats pass beneath each day.

The next morning, you walk into the city room and tell the city editor, "I have a darned good feature. If you can get a photographer out to the drawbridge for a shot of the operator, I'll have a story this morning on the loneliest job in town."

The city editor approves your suggestion, so you begin your story:

> John C. Dalton has the loneliest job in town.
>
> Each day, hundreds of people pass within 15 feet of Dalton, but no one says "hello", or even gives a friendly wave.
>
> Dalton, 64, of 801 Ninth Street, has been the city's drawbridge operator for 40 solitary years.
>
> "Nobody ever pays attention to me except when the bridge is up," Dalton said, with a sad grin. "Then, while they wait on the barge to pass, they honk their horns and cuss.
>
> "It's not a bad job, but it sure gets lonesome."

The story continues with more quotes from Dalton, description of his appearance and mannerisms, anecdotes from his 40-year career, and explanation of the workings of the draw bridge.

The city editor reads your story, nods approvingly, and passes it to the copy desk for editing and headline writing. It is a classic feature story by definition:

A feature story is a creative, sometimes subjective, article designed primarily to entertain and to inform readers of an event, a situation or an aspect of life.

It is often not perishable—it can be held for days or weeks before being printed. It has no established limits of length. It allows for descriptive and stylish techniques that are banned from newswriting, and it may not have any news value.

A veteran newsman once described a feature story more succinctly: "A feature story is anything that isn't a news story." With few exceptions, his definition is correct.

Let's examine the definition point by point:

Creativity

Unlike news writing, feature writing allows a reporter to create a story virtually at will.

Although still bound by the ethics of accuracy—fiction is categorically banned—a reporter can conjure a feature story in his imagination and, after researching his idea, write it.

For example, a general assignment reporter may be assigned feature coverage for the Christmas season. While he may see and write several feature stories based on events such as "living nativity scenes," Christmas parties for underpriveleged children, etc., the reporter may soon look for the "different angle."

He may decide to play Santa Claus at a department store. After donning red suit and beard, the reporter listens to dozens of children requesting gifts, carefully observes the reactions of children to Santa, and remembers the problems that a store Santa encounters.

He may survey Christmas tree lots to watch the strange rituals of tree-buyers and chat with lot operators about how to pick a good tree.

The results are good, entertaining feature stories that budded in the reporter's mind and blossomed in print.

Subjectivity

Some feature stories are written in the first person, thus allowing the reporter to inject his own emotions and thoughts. Although many reporters who are trained in objective reporting use this technique only when there is no alternative, the result can be very readable and entertaining.

Reporters enjoy adventures and experiences while seeking news stories that sometimes lend themselves to this style. If, for example, a reporter is kidnapped by a mental patient and rescued after a long ordeal, his thoughts, observations and personal experiences can make a thrilling feature story.

Young reporters should, however, be cautioned against the "ego trip" pitfall. A common mistake among new reporters is the tendency to seek to "make a name for myself" through first person reporting.

Few editors will permit the over-use of this technique because subjectivity can become a "crutch" used to avoid strong descriptive writing that is the mark of a good feature writer. Many veterans use this guideline: Unless you are the main protagonist in the story, leave yourself out of it.

Informativeness

A feature story, while lacking in hard news value, can constructively inform the public of a situation or aspect of life that may escape coverage in hard news stories.

Your city may have a valuable institution that is in danger of closing for lack of funding—a museum of natural history, for example.

A reporter may visit the museum to interview the director about the financial crisis. The result of the interview could be a small news item with a headline: "Natural History Museum Operates in the Red."

But the reporter may see a different angle that turns the news story into a page-one feature. Children at the museum are obviously intrigued by the menagerie of animals. Here's the story he wrote:

> Grumpy Mr. Groundhog stared balefully at the small hand that poked his fluffy fur, and ignored the giggles of delight from the dozen children who gathered around him.
>
> Mr. Groundhog may not have to put up with such irritations much longer. The Museum of Natural History may soon close for lack of funds.

The reporter concentrated on capturing interaction between the children and the animals. He described the joy of the children and the love and care with which they treated the animals.

The result? The museum was saved by a flood of timely contributions, large and small, from throughout the city.

Many readers weren't aware of the museum's plight. Others weren't aware of the services it provided to the community. Because of the story, citizens decided that it was an institution worth keeping, so they chipped in to save it.

The informative aspect of feature writing can take many other forms. A feature story can often translate the impact of a disaster into human terms by focusing on the plight of people affected by the disaster. Social conditions, such as ghetto housing, can be effectively publicized with good descriptive feature writing. Voters can gain valuable insight to political candidates through accurate, probing personal profiles.

While many features are light and breezy, the feature can be a profound tool in the hands of a competent writer. A feature story can appeal to the best of human instincts to bring about constructive change.

Entertainment

In the past two decades, the feature story has become an important tool in newspapers' efforts to compete with electronic media. The feature story is a big, extra dividend that newspapers can offer its readers.

Newspaper reporters quickly admit that they can't "beat" electronics media newsmen in reaching the public with a story first. Radio and television newsmen can air a major story within minutes after facts are known.

But the newspaper reporter knows that his readers won't see his story until hours after the event, when the newspaper is delivered at their doorsteps. He may beat his broadcast rivals with exclusive news stories, but once news media are generally aware of a story, he can provide a more in-depth version of the story his readers heard on radio.

With this in mind, reporters on even the most active news beats are constantly looking for feature stories. A feature story is normally exclusive, so there's no chance of being beaten by electronic media or newspaper rivals. It also provides a means of making friends on the beat—a feature story subject is a reporter's friend for life.

The feature gives a welcome break in the monotony of murder, scandal, disaster, and controversy which comprise much of the hard news. It can give the newspaper reader something to chuckle about, a diversion of escapism.

A reporter may write a "color story" aimed at capturing the mood and atmosphere of the opening game of the World Series. He chats with a 90-year-old great-grandmother. He talks with a police officer, a soda pop vender, the wife of a star pitcher and a gate crasher. The result is a highly entertaining story about people which effectively puts the reader in a choice seat for the spectacle.

A police reporter may collect dozens of funny anecdotes about police experiences over a period of months and, on a slow news day, he may write a funny feature story on police humor—the lighter side of a dangerous job.

A city hall reporter, covering a city council meeting, may write a separate feature story capturing the humor of behind-the-scenes politicking at the meeting.

The education beat reporter may attend the first day of school in a first grade class to write a feature on the varied reactions of children to their first experience with school.

In each case, the primary objective is to entertain the reader and give him another good reason to subscribe to your newspaper.

Unperishable

According to an old newspaper adage, yesterday's newspaper is only good for wrapping fish. The all-important news element fades into history within 24 hours. A reporter may work under extreme deadline pressure—and sometimes physical danger—to shake loose an important story or cover a tense situation. Yet, once deadline is passed and the story is filed, his city editor quickly asks what he may have for tomorrow.

While news stories are highly perishable, feature stories may be kept for days, weeks, or months. Many smaller newspapers try to build a bank of "overset copy"—mostly features. The stories are set into type and stored in the composing room for a slow day, because the editor knows that the value of the story won't diminish with time.

Perhaps the unperishable nature of features can be considered still another way. Many wiley veterans keep a list of feature ideas for slow weeks. The theory is that by having ripe features handy, they can impress their editors with consistent production. Some reporters even complete necessary research and keep their notes handy for "instant features."

From the reporter's viewpoint, the feature offers still another important advantage: deadline pressure is rare, so a reporter can take sufficient time to fully research a feature and rewrite it as much as necessary to get maximum quality.

A major, in-depth feature may require several days' work. A personal profile on the local police chief may entail lengthy interviews with friends, co-workers, family, and enemies as well as with the chief. The reporter may spend several days with the chief to observe his mannerisms, reactions to given situations, and idiosyncracies.

In writing the story, the reporter may type out a rough draft, rewrite it, edit it, rewrite it again and again until he is satisfied. The city editor may suggest changes and require still another rewrite. The story is slowly polished into a fine, professional feature. And during the long process, no one has worried about the time element.

Length

If a reporter asks a city editor how long a given news story should be, the city editor will probably reply, "as short as you can make it." A good news story is an orderly rendition of relevant facts, arranged to promote quick and easy readership. The news story is written with facts given in decreasing order of importance so that a copy editor merely snips from the bottom if the story is too long.

If a reporter asks how long a feature story should be, the editor may reply, "as long as you keep it interesting."

Feature stories vary in length from two or three paragraphs to 15 or 20 triple-spaced sheets of copy. Reader interest is the main yardstick by which they are judged. And editors are paid to accurately assess reader interest.

The lack of guidelines on length should by no means be interpreted as an incentive to write long, rambling stories. A good feature writer is aware that irrelevant "flab" and unnecessary verbiage will lessen the chances of the story reaching print and, should it be printed, readers will become bored quickly and jump to another story.

The writer also knows that the editing of a feature story is a delicate process. Because feature stories have endings, a copy editor cannot whack from the bottom. Material must be painstakingly deleted, word by word, line by line.

So it is in the writer's interest to write concisely and stick to the subject. If a copy editor arbitrarily chops out a key paragraph, the rambling writer must share the blame.

WRITING TECHNIQUES

While a news story is concerned only with the rendition of facts, a feature story allows for true story-telling techniques. In the final analysis, that is a key difference between a hard news story and a feature story: The feature writer is basically a story-teller.

As a story-teller, the feature writer paints pictures with words; he conjures images in the mind of the reader, he draws the reader into the story by helping him to identify with the protagonist.

If a city hall reporter describes the mayor from his glossy black patent leather shoes to his frosty white mustache in a news story, the city editor would go into a rage because of his verbosity. Yet if the same reporter omitted such description from a feature story about the mayor, the city editor may say, "What does he look like? I can't 'see' him."

A feature writer is a pragmatist. He uses basic journalistic writing techniques for the most part, because he knows that they are effective in communicating. But if a rule should detract from his ability to tell the story, he quickly discards it.

The inverted pyramid is often ignored when the sequence of events naturally builds into a good story. "Brights"—short, humorous features often found on page one—are frequently written in sequential order:

Patrolman Richard Jackson had the worst night of his career Friday.

At 4:30 p.m., he reported to work. Five minutes later, during a uniform inspection, he dropped his nightstick. Bending over to pick it up, he ripped the seat of his pants.

At 5:15 p.m., he responded to a barking dog complaint. A half hour later, he was treated for a dog bite on the leg at County Medical Center.

Shortly after 7 p.m., Jackson pulled over a speeding car on Main Street. The driver was a narcotics detective who was following a suspected heroin dealer.

At 9:50 p.m., he was called to a bar to break up a fight. A half hour later, he was treated for cuts and bruises at County Medical Center after being hit over the head with a bottle of whiskey.

Jackson returned to the Medical Center at 11:40 p.m., after he ran into a neck-high clothesline while chasing a burglary suspect. His right leg was cut by glass when he fell.

Leaving the Medical Center, he was returning to police headquarters at 12:05 a.m. to end the day when another motorist drove into the rear end of Jackson's cruiser at a stop light. For once, Jackson wasn't injured.

Finally, at 12:30 a.m. Jackson limped out of police headquarters to go home. When he reached the parking lot, he found yet another crime to report:

Stolen: A 1973 Buick Sedan, Licensed JG-805.

Owner: Richard Jackson, 31, of 2126 Grove Drive.

The reporter who chose to write about Patrolman Jackson's misadventures in a sequential, feature fashion rather than as a hard news story gained considerable mileage from the available material. The feature story has page one potential, while a news story may not even see the light of print. Realistically, a news story would be like this:

Patrolman Richard Jackson was treated for minor injuries received in three separate incidents Friday night. The officer was also involved in a minor automobile accident.

Jackson, 31, was bitten by a dog at 5:15 p.m.: struck on the head by a whiskey bottle in a bar at 9:50 p.m.; and slashed on the leg by broken glass when he fell during a chase at 11:27 p.m. He was treated and released at County Medical Center after each incident.

Jake Smith, 38, of 19 Main Street was arrested and charged with assault and battery on a police officer in the bar altercation.

Jackson's cruiser received minor damage when it was struck in the rear by a car driven by Mrs. June Riley at the intersection of Math Street and Clover Avenue at 12:05 a.m. today. No one was injured.

Note that while the news story contains more information about the incidents covered in the story, it does not include un-newsworthy, but interesting material such as the ripped pants or the stopping of the narcotics detective. The reporter could easily justify leaving out the stolen car incident because it is a separate incident not directly related to his story that deals with injuries and near injuries to a policeman.

Which story is more interesting? Which story is more informative? Which story was more fun to write for the reporter?

In comparing the two stories, it is easy to see why most reporters are constantly alert for feature angles.

EXERCISES

Clip a feature story from the local newspaper and analyze it as follows:

1. What is the basic story line?
2. Why is it worth reading? What purpose does it serve?
3. Could it have been written as a news story? If so, why wasn't it? If not, why not?
4. Is it creative? If so, how?
5. Is it subjective?
6. Is it informative?
7. Is it entertaining?
8. Is it unperishable?
9. Are any stylish or descriptive writing techniques used?
10. Can you deduce from the story how the reporter gathered the information?
11. Was the story complete? Is there additional information you wish had been included?
12. Did the reporter include material that isn't relevant?

2 Accuracy: The Mark of Professionalism

A feature writer certainly needs a fertile imagination to weave words and phrases into crisp, gripping stories. But, as with other forms of journalism, the writer's imagination must not color the factual content of the story.

In short, fiction is not allowed in feature writing.

The temptation to fudge a little is often strong, particularly when there's little likelihood that the falsehood will be discovered. But a professional journalist shrugs off the tendency because he is acutely aware of the ethics and the dangers involved.

The ethics are based on the scruple that opinions and fiction are expressly banned from all but special sections of the newspaper. The editorial page, of course, provides outlet for opinions and it is clearly labeled as opinionated material. Many newspapers publish Sunday magazines and other special sections that allow clearly labeled fiction.

A feature story isn't supposed to be fiction, so any "coloring" of facts will deceive the readers. When such a deception becomes known, the credibility of the newspaper would suffer greatly. Feature stories run beside news stories, so readers would wonder, with justification, whether so-called news stories also had fictitious elements.

There are several degrees of fiction writing, as applied to feature stories. The most obvious is the creation of an entire story using fabricated material. Perhaps very few reporters would have the gall to try to slip such a story past a crusty city editor.

The greatest temptation occurs when the writer is on the verge of having a good feature, yet a few elements are missing. He can possibly acquire the needed elements by convincing the subject of the story to enliven his tale. He becomes a co-conspirator in the selling of a fraudulent story.

Still another technique is the art of putting quotes into the subject's mouth. The reporter prefaces the suggested quote with, "Would you say that . . ." and waits for a nod of confirmation—either real or imagined.

Obviously, a few unethical reporters are loose in the newspaper world, but, like habitual liars, they live in fear of exposure and subsequent unemployment or ostracism by their ethical colleagues.

As you will see as we progress, legitimate feature stories are so plentiful and easy to find that there is never a justification or a reason for resorting to fiction.

From a selfish viewpoint, a reporter knows that his reputation is vital to his success. Any reporter who is loose with facts will soon find that no news source will provide information. Since very few newspapers hire reporters exclusively for feature writing, the reporter who sacrifices accuracy for a good feature story may find himself in deep trouble when covering news beat events.

GETTING INFORMATION CORRECT

Most inaccuracies that get into print result from carelessness rather than from intent. A reporter may not take sufficient time to check his information before writing a feature story. Later, he finds that he misspelled the subject's name.

A veteran reporter will take the same precautions to avoid factual errors in a feature story that he takes when writing a complicated news story:

1. Whenever you interview someone, ask his name, age, address and telephone number. After scribbling down the information, spell the name aloud and read off his address and telephone number so that the subject can verify the information. The telephone number is not included in the story, but a reporter should take it as a means of contacting the subject.

2. If the name, age and address are acquired second hand, check the city directory or telephone directory. If you use the age, call the subject to verify.

3. Never assume you know something. Always doublecheck pertinent information. For example, a city hall reporter may assume he knows the official title of a city bureaucrat. But if he isn't certain, he should call the official or his secretary to verify it.

4. If your story deals with complicated material, make sure you understand it. A reporter often finds himself writing about a technical field in which he has no background.

Perhaps a police reporter is doing a feature on radar equipment used in traffic control. A police captain may easily rattle off vast technical explanations of radar operation, but the reporter must be able to write a clear explanation for mass consumption. So the veteran police reporter will repeatedly interrupt the captain to seek a clear, layman's translation of technical gobbledygook.

Many reporters operate by the rule of thumb: "If I can understand it, anyone can understand it." In using this guideline, the reporter becomes a "devil's advocate" for his readers. He assumes the role of the average newspaper reader and questions his source accordingly.

5. When using statistics or mathematical data, the reporter should check figures and arithmetic. Of the thousands of people who read the article, some will be accountants, engineers and other professionals who deal with mathematics. Many reporters have squirmed with embarrassment when an astute reader spotted inaccurate arithmetic and wrote a letter pointing out the error.

Statistics should be especially suspect. It has been said that you can prove anything with statistics, depending on how you present them and what you include or omit. Question the source carefully to ascertain the soundness of the figures.

For example, police crime statistics are notoriously unreliable as indicators of crime. Many officers explain that numerous crimes are not reported to police, thus there is no way for a police department to account for all crimes. Also, some police departments have been found intentionally shading crime statistics to create a crime decrease for public relations reasons, or a crime increase when the department seeks more manpower.

A reporter must not allow himself to be used as a means of deceiving the public. Astute questioning and sound checking can often prevent such deception.

Spelling and Word Use

"Words are the tools of the trade. If you can't spell correctly or use words effectively and accurately, you don't belong in the newspaper business."

This admonition came from an angry city editor who has discovered several misspelled words in a young reporter's story. The reporter took the message seriously and, from that day on, used his dictionary religiously.

Many young reporters have wished that they had taken the warning of their professors more seriously. Spelling is not a mere academic exercise designed to bedevil students. Spelling is a *must* for survival in the competitive world of journalism.

Few reporters could win spelling bees, but almost all reporters can —and do—read dictionaries. Even under deadline pressure, a visitor to the city room of a newspaper can see hands darting repeatedly for dictionaries.

The city editor's concern has pragmatic roots. Thousands and thousands of words are processed by the copy desk each day. Although copy editors are responsible for catching errors in stories, it is humanly impossible for them to catch every error. So, the city editor must continuously seek to catch such errors at the source: the reporter's typewriters.

If a spelling error appears in print, several things can happen— none of them is good:

The credibility of the newspaper suffers. Spelling errors detract from the professional image of newspapers and make their content suspect to astute readers who catch the errors. If a newspaper is careless with words, how can facts be trusted?

The credibility of the reporter suffers for the same reason. Libel can result, especially if names are misspelled. If the pattern of misspellings is repeated too often the editor may fire the reporter for professional incompetence.

Misuse of words can have similar repercussions. Most people frequently misuse words daily during conversations because they picked up a word fully understanding its meaning. Conversational misuses are excusable and understandable, but all excuses cease when a reporter misuses a word in print.

Woe be to the reporter who files a story with this sentence: "The mayor inferred that a tax increase may be considered at Monday night's council meeting." To infer means to deduce or conclude from evidence. It does not mean "imply."

If a city editor seeks high standards of professionalism, he may nitpick at even the most marginal misuses. Attribution is a common ground for arguments between editors and reporters. "He said" versus "He says" has filled many a city room with angry words.

"But that's what he says," the reporter argues.

"Did he say it only once, or does he continue to say it?" the city editor asks.

"He said it only once, but that's his official position," the reporter replies.

"If he repeats the quotation at every opportunity, you may use 'he says,' but if he said it only once, use 'he said.'" The city editor rules.

Some cases of word misuse are far more serious. There is a story of a young reporter who was writing a feature about an unusual elderly woman who kept an unusual house. Her huge, rambling man-

elderly woman who kept an unusual house. Her huge, rambling mansion was furnished with oriental furniture and fixtures. To add to the atmosphere, she burned incense.

The reporter groped for the right word when he attempted to describe the aroma. "The house reeked with incest," he declared.

Other easy-to-misuse words can greatly alter the meaning of a story. "A federal mediator was called in to arbitrate the dispute between the union and management," a story reads.

While many people don't know that, by definition, a mediator cannot arbitrate, members of labor unions are acutely aware of the difference. The difference between mediation and arbitration can greatly affect the contract that will result.

The consequences of word misuse can be grave:

Libel can easily result. The woman whose home "reeked with incest" may have an excellent chance of recovering damages in a libel suit.

The reputation of the newspaper can be severely damaged. Union members who spot the contradiction of the mediator's arbitration will certainly have less esteem for the offending newspaper.

The reporter's reputation can suffer greatly. In future labor negotiations, officials on both sides may have little respect for him and as a result, give him little information. Readers will question the accuracy of stories printed under his by-line.

Unemployment is often the result of a lost libel suit.

STYLEBOOK USE

Most newspapers require reporters to adhere to rules listed in a stylebook. The stylebook, which may be published by the newspaper or by a wire service, specifies how words, titles and dates must be used to insure uniformity.

The Associated Press and United Press International have agreed on a common list of style rules which are widely used.

There are several reasons for having and using stylebooks:

1. Uniform usage is simply more professional in appearance.

2. When a word is presented in several different—but correct—forms, many readers will mistakenly conclude that only one is correct and that the reporter obviously erred. For example, per cent can also be used as percent, per-cent or %.

3. Most style usages are designed to save space. Space is a valuable premium on a newspaper.

4. Uniform style saves time. A reporter who learns stylebook

usage doesn't need to hesitate to consider which form to use. Under deadline pressure, hesitation can be costly.

If a stylebook is required, use it with the same rigidity as you use the dictionary. An error, whether in style or spelling, detracts from your professional image.

Catching Those Errors

Every reporter uses some system to catch spelling, style and word-use errors. Those who are gifted with a talent for spelling may need only a quick once-over to correct errors, but other reporters develop elaborate systems to check their work.

The following is one such system:

Do not check for spelling, style or word-use while writing the story. The constant interruption of using the dictionary and stylebook will break your creative flow and require more time.

Once the story is written, however, check over the story word by word. View each word as a possible "enemy" that can sabotage your story. When there is even a remote possibility that the word is wrong, check it.

If time permits check over it quickly once again. Frequently, your eyes will skip a line or a paragraph when you check your story. An indication of this is when errors appear in groups. The second check should lessen the chance of this happening.

On some feature stories, you may have several days to work on the story before it must be turned in. In such cases, let the story sit for a day or so *after* your systematic check. Then, before handing it in, sift through it still another time. With a fresh outlook, errors are sometimes more obvious.

When you discover a misspelled or misused word, write it down. Some reporters keep lists of troublesome words for quick and handy reference. It also helps in learning to spell them correctly.

Under deadline pressure, reporters often resort to safe synonyms when unsure of the correct spelling. If time permits, look up the correct spelling for that "just right" word. If it's impossible, then use an alternate word.

EXERCISE 1

In the following feature story, there are several misspelled and misused words. Use your dictionary to check this copy and make corrections as needed.

Who ever swiped a green, 1974 Mustang parked in front of Capitol City Police Headquarters last night may be in deep troble.

"I'm droping every other case to give this one my full attention," said detective William O'Donnel of the auto theft squod." I will definitely arest someone for this one."

"O'Donnel, who has won the reputation as the ace of the auto theft squod after solving 89 per cent of his cases this year, admits taking a personnel intrest in last night's theft.

On the police report, the case seems routine: stolen auto: a 1974 Mustang, dark green, license XU 987. Reported stolen from parking lot at 333 W. Third St. between 3 P.M. and 4:30 P.M.

But the reson for O'Donnel's interest is found on the top line of the report. "Owner" William P. O'Donnel, 32, of 1604 Eithg Avenu South.

"He can consider himself cought," O'Donnel declared. "And when I find the car, there had beter not be a scrach on it."

EXERCISE 2

Listed below are 50 commonly misspelled words. Some are correct and some are misspelled. Correct those that are misspelled. Do not use a dictionary. After completing the exercise, consult your dictionary.

Ignorance	Interupt
Tremendous	Argueing
Omision	Metalic
Phenomenon	Suppression
Acknowlédge	Separately
Referred	Incredable
Exhuberant	Noticable
Acquainted	Abreviate
Observent	Subsidary
Recurence	Absorption
Literaly	Vicious
Accidently	Leisure
Responsible	Infallable
Privilege	Seize
Miscelaneous	Occasionally
Wheather	Disappoint
Comparatively	Arrained
	Nonchalant
Convenience	Prepondrance
Superintendant	Acrue
Permanent	Permissable
Successful	Disastrous
Vengance	Preceeding
Sustenence	Verbiage
Accomodate	Hypocrisy

3 Feature Leads

The key to writing a good feature story lies in the first paragraph —the lead. Trying to capture a reader's interest without a good lead is like fishing with a bare hook.

Every reporter is acutely aware of the importance of a lead. Wastebaskets are filled with sub-standard leads, as reporters search for that just-right arrangement of words that will draw readers into his story.

The feature lead has two vital objectives:

To draw the readers into the story.
To set the stage for the material to follow.

The reporter has a wide repertoire of leads to choose from, some are designed to startle and shock the reader, others to tickle his curiosity, others to stir his imagination, and still others to succinctly inform him about the nature of the story.

Reporters are pragmatists who rarely are aware of the type of lead they write. Their total concentration is directed toward finding that elusive combination of words. But, for learning purposes, the student journalist should know and experiment with various leads, such as the following:

THE SUMMARY LEAD

The summary lead is essentially the same as that used in most hard news stories. It gives the gist of the story and lets the reader decide if he is interested enough in the subject to read the rest.

Summary leads are most often used when the reporter has a strong, interesting subject that will sell itself. Because the summary lead is the easiest to write, many reporters fall back on it when they are under deadline pressure, or when they are stymied in searching for a better lead.

Here are some examples of summary leads:

> Charles and Louise Taylor have been living in a 1964 Ford since he lost his job two weeks ago. They are out of money and almost out of gas.
>
> Building a soap box derby car isn't an easy job for Johnny Sanders, 11, who has been paralyzed from waist down for five years.
>
> Police Chief Joe Smith's Baptist upbringing and his youthful fling at gambling have combined to make him a deadly foe of Capitol City's gamblers.

Notice that in each example, the gist of the story to follow is crisply stated in the lead. The reader knows, after reading the first lead, that the story is about a family in deep trouble. The second lead quickly informs the reader that the story is about a courageous lad who is competing in a race despite his handicap. The third lead informs readers that the story will be about the police chief's fight against city gamblers.

The stories have one thing in common: They are strong feature subjects which should interest most readers. The reporter can forego sales pitches and let the stories sell themselves.

The Narrative Lead

The narrative lead, a favorite with fiction writers, puts the reader into the story and draws him through it. The technique is to create a situation and skillfully let the reader become the protagonist, either by leaving a vacuum which the reader mentally fills or by allowing him to identify with a person in the midst of the action.

The result of the technique is closely akin to that of a good movie. Have you every become thirsty during a movie in which the hero gropes through desert mirages? Have you trembled in your seat during a horror movie?

Narrative leads are especially effective in telling adventure stories. Perhaps a mountain climber flopped helplessly at the end of a rope for hours before he was rescued.

> Craggy boulders loomed menacingly 200 feet below as Charles Summers swung helplessly on the end of a rope that dangled along a sheer cliff, in a buffeting wind, on the north side of Adams Peak.

Police reporters often use narrative leads in feature stories about police actions.

> The red tail lights ahead slowly grew smaller as Detective Dan Baker floored the accelerator of his unmarked cruiser, pushing the speedometer needle past 90, in an effort to catch the fleeing Cadillac.

Another police feature may begin:

> Patrolman William Easton gazed nervously into the barrel of the 12-gauge shotgun, then jumped aside with cat-like quickness as he pushed the barrel down and fired his revolver.

The advantage of narrative lead is that it can captivate a reader better than any other lead. Once the reader identifies with—or becomes—the protagonist, he is hopelessly hooked.

The disadvantage is that few stories naturally lend themselves to narrative leads. Reporters who try to force a narrative lead onto a story may find that the lead is either flat and unnatural, or that the lead greatly distorts the story.

THE DESCRIPTIVE LEAD

A descriptive lead conjures a mental picture of the subject or site for the reader. While applicable to many types of features, the descriptive lead is a favorite for many reporters in writing personal profiles.

While a narrative lead puts the reader in the middle of the action, the descriptive lead places him a few feet away, in a position to see, hear, and smell.

The artful use of adjectives is the key to a descriptive lead. A good reporter can make the subject "come alive." The subject seems to rise from the cold black print.

The reporter often tries to focus on one element of the subject that best illustrates it.

> The cold gray eyes narrow to a squint as they probe a face and seem to penetrate into the hidden recesses of the mind in search of a lie.

> They are the eyes of a cop.

For many readers, the lead could be chilling. The cold, gray eyes of the police officer are staring up at them as they read.

Human subjects aren't always necessary. Inanimate objects can also have a "personality" that can be effectively captured by a good descriptive lead.

> The haunting whispers of Confederate soldiers and the sad singing of slaves seem to hang in the air around the 130-year-old mansion that rises from knee-high weeds in the blistering Alabama sun.

The descriptive lead can be an effective caricature, like an artist's line-sketch, which emphasizes key features, ignoring uninteresting detail.

> Woolly black eyebrows, a leonine mane of white hair, and a sulky scowl give city councilman Paul Edwards the look of an avenging angel as he glowers at hapless city employees from his council chair each Monday night.

Or, a descriptive lead can quickly endow the subject with interesting characteristics by describing an appropriate setting.

> Judge Carl Miller grimly leaned forward to peer down from his towering bench to examine the face of a perspiring young lawyer who was desperately searching for legal straws to save his client.

A descriptive lead can also capture an overall, birdseye view of a scene.

> A sea of white shirts and dresses sprinkled with red caps and pennants rippled in eddies toward hot dog stands as the World Series opened Sunday in Cincinnati's Riverfront Stadium.

Perhaps the most difficult descriptive lead to write is the blurred action effect. The reader is not informed of the subject, but, instead, is barraged with seemingly disjointed description. The result is a feeling of dizzy action—like an eerie dream.

> Green, white and red lights whizzed by in dazzling lines that soon blurred and blended with nightmarish thunder overhead.

In the example above, the reporter was describing the dizzy visual effect of riding down an airport runway in an airport security car. He quickly placed the readers' feet on the ground by explaining the situation in the second paragraph.

> The psychodelic world of airport runways and thundering jets is part of an often boring routine to airport security policeman Edward Seeley.

When examining the endless possibilities for descriptive leads, it's easy to see why many reporters are "hooked" on descriptive leads.

THE QUOTATION LEAD

A profound, succinct quote can make an interesting lead, particularly when the speaker is well known in the community. The quote should give insight to the character of the speaker.

Remember, the lead must set the stage for the story to follow, so the quotation should focus on the nature of your story.

An example of a quotation lead is:

> "The people, my friend, are a great beast," writer H. L. Mencken snarled.

Mencken, as you may know, was a great cynic who gleefully burst balloons of human egocentrism. Such a quotation lead would both grab the interest of the reader and give insight to Mencken.

The great disadvantage of quotation leads is that the quotation chosen may be naturally distorted and yanked out of context because of the great emphasis given to it in the lead.

Let's say you are interviewing the mayor. While most of his comments are favorable toward his job, he may mutter, at a bad moment, "This is a rotten job."

The quotation would be an eye-catcher, so a reporter may be tempted to use it in the lead. But the quotation does not accurately reflect the mayor's overall expressed feelings toward the office. And, unless the reporter informs the reader of the circumstances during which he made the remark, the quotation would be totally out of context.

THE QUESTION LEAD

A question lead can be effective if it succeeds in challenging the reader's knowledge or curiosity.

Too often, the question lead is used as a backup by a reporter who can't quite create an imaginative lead. It is easy to write, but is rarely the best possible lead.

In most cases, the questions are gimmicks. The reporter knows very well that the readers can't know the answer. Yet he is whitting their curiosity for the subject of the story.

Many editors frown on such gimmick leads because they are often crutches and because readers often resent being tricked into reading a story. A strong narrative or descriptive lead is usually preferred.

Question leads should not, however, be categorically dismissed as inferior. Occasionally, a story will provide a natural vehicle for a question lead.

Baseball fans may recall the 1972 World Series in which Cincinnati's star catcher Johnny Bench saw a third strike whiz by after the Oakland catcher signaled for an intentional walk on a three ball and two strike count. A clever sportswriter, writing a sidebar feature, may use this lead:

> What's the best way to strike out an all-star catcher?
> Oakland pitcher Jim "Catfish" Hunter believes there's no substitute for subterfuge.

A city hall reporter who writes a feature on a citizen's efforts to overcome city hall bureaucracy may write:

> Is there a way to beat city hall?

As with other leads, the question lead can be effective only when the story material lends itself *naturally* to such a lead.

The Direct Address Lead

When the reporter communicates directly to the reader, it is called a direct address lead. Almost invariably, the direct address lead is characterized by the word "you" inserted somewhere in the first paragraph, or implied.

The advantage is obvious. The reader—sometimes involuntarily—becomes part of the story. The wording implies that there's something in the story for *you,* personally.

A reporter, who has researched city laws for obscure and unenforced laws, may write:

> So you think you're a law-abiding citizen. Maybe. But chances are that you have broken the law several times today.

Such a lead would be hard to ignore because the reader has been personally challenged, and because human curiosity has been strongly pricked.

The lead is obviously a gimmick, but the subject matter probably requires an imaginative sales pitch. It is unlikely that a descriptive lead could effectively capture a collection of obscure laws. No action is available for a narrative lead. A summary lead is possible, but not a particularly exciting prospect. A quotation lead may be applicable, as could a question lead. But, by process of elimination, a direct address lead is a superior choice.

The danger of direct address leads is that they can easily become heavy-handed or amateurish. Witness:

> Did you know that rainbow trout aren't native to the famed Colorado streams where fishermen flock from all over the country?

With the possible exception of rainbow trout, who cares? The lead is desperately forced and downright corny.

THE TEASER LEAD

A teaser lead is a device to deceive readers in a jesting manner. The total objective is to grab the reader's curiosity and gently lead him into the story.

Teaser leads are generally very short, crisp, and light. Riddles are frequently used. The teaser lead gives the reader little or no insight to the nature of the story to follow:

> It has 200 legs, a thousand toes, a hundred noses, and scores of horns.

Obviously, the reader has no real clue to the nature of the strange beast described. The reporter is setting the reader up for a feature about a marching band—not a weird insect or monster.

A fragment of a fact may be dangled enticingly under the reader's nose to snare him:

> She said "no" but she did it anyway.

The reader can interpret this lead many ways, some of which do not belong in a family newspaper. The reporter wants the reader to think the worst so that he can happily finish the set up with the second paragraph punchline:

For 10 years, Donna Mae Fowler, 71, had spurned marriage proposals from Charles Farley, 77. Yesterday, she still said "no," but Farley simply turned off his hearing aid and drove to the home of Justice of the Peace Paul Miller.

Miss Fowler said "no" once more as they entered, but she changed her plea in the middle of the ceremony. She emerged as Mrs. Charles Farley.

"She was just being cantankerous," Farley said, chuckling.

The teaser is very similar to a television news lead-in. On many stations, a newsman appears during station break before the news program to tease the viewer into tuning in.

"He said he wouldn't, but he did," a television newsman said during such a break on the day that former Vice President Spiro Agnew resigned.

THE FREAK LEAD

Lettuce is green
Milk is white
Food prices are going
    out of sight.

An imaginative—if unpoetic—reporter may try such a lead in writing a zany feature story about soaring food prices. The lead is catchy and informative. Its unusual, non-conformist style may attract readers and sell the story.

Freak leads are the most extreme gimmicks. Yet, the sheer brazenness of the lead may hook the reader—if the reporter can follow his first act with a zany, lively story. The tone of the lead is very hard to sustain throughout a story.

Some newspapers refuse to carry freak leads for good reasons. Reporters live in a world of words. As a result, many newsmen are incurable punsters. Only a rigid policy can prevent a deluge of imaginative puns and rhymes from engulfing readers.

Nevertheless, freak leads are just as natural in some stories as descriptive or narrative leads are in others.

Imagine a reporter gathering material for a feature story on an Old West cemetery. What would make a better lead than a colorful epitaph from a gunfighter's grave?

Freaks can also take the form of one word leads.

KAAAAABOOOOOOOM!

The cannon belched a cloud of thick, black smoke as it weakly coughed out a cannon ball for the first time since the Battle of Gettysburg.

Or, the freak lead may tell about the weather:

OOOPS!

That's the word today, as Capitol City folks woke up this morning to discover the icy present from last night's winter storm.

COMBINATION LEADS

Many leads you see in your newspaper combine two or more types of leads, using the best elements of each.

Quotation leads are often combined with descriptive leads.

"I never stole a cent of public money," Mayor Richard Jackson shouted as he wiped tears from his eyes and mopped beads of perspiration from his brow.

A teaser lead may be combined with a quotation.

"My word, what is that?"

"Is it one of ours?"

"I hope it doesn't crash!"

Hundreds of Capitol City citizens echoed these comments Monday when the flying circus came to town.

WRITING LEADS

Once a reporter chooses the lead topic and selects his basic approach, he faces the problem of choosing the best combination of words.

Regardless of how imaginative and interesting his idea for a lead may be, he can still fail to grab readers' attention if he writes a poor combination of words.

Remember the descriptive lead used on the story about a policeman?

The cold grey eyes narrow to a squint as they probe a face and seem to penetrate into the hidden recesses of the mind in search of a lie. They are the eyes of a cop.

The same idea could have been poorly executed by a less capable reporter to produce this drowsy, wordy lead:

Detective William Smith has somewhat cold, grey eyes that have a way of looking at a person so that it seems that they go into the deep part of the mind to see what you're really thinking. Detective Smith has that cold-eyed look that sort of seems unique among policemen.

Compare the two leads. The idea is the same. The leads say essentially the same thing. But the first lead is effective and succinct, while the second lead would attract few people other than Detective Smith's immediate family.

If you closely analyze the leads, the following guidelines for lead writing become obvious:

Be succinct

Don't waste words. The second lead is about 50 per cent longer than the first example. Despite its greater length, the second lead gives no more basic information than the first, other than the name of the officer.

Unnecessary verbiage dilutes the effectiveness of the lead, in the same way that a good, thick broth becomes a thin soup when too much water is added.

When a lead is boiled down to essential, interesting words, each word carries impact.

Write a short paragraph

Many professionals use this rule of thumb: No more than four lines (not sentences) to a lead. A short paragraph simply appears more inviting. Words stand out better, and it's easier to read.

As you will see in subsequent chapters, journalists arbitrarily break off paragraphs when they become too long. Many reporters search for a place to end the paragraph after 2½ lines. Forget the rules of English composition: A formal essay is a thing of beauty, but the half-page long paragraphs would create a long, gray, unreadable monster in print.

Use action words

A lead must have life and energy. A reader must feel a sense of movement as he reads it.

The feature writer avoids passive verb tenses because the active tense is normally shorter and more exciting. The verb is the sparkplug: It provides energy to give your lead life.

Adjectives can also provide needed glitter. The choice of bright, colorful adjectives will do the same for your lead as a bright, colorful dress will do for a pretty girl: It enhances vitality.

Let's see how adjectives, verbs, and even adverbs can combine to add energy. Remember this lead?:

> Green, white, and red lights whizzed by in dazzling lines that soon blurred and blended with nightmarish thunder overhead.

The subject—green, white, and red lights—is bright and colorful. The verb—whizzed—is zestful. Action words are carefully sprinkled throughout the rest of the lead to weave a lively image:

> . . . dazzling lines . . . blurred and blended . . . .nightmarish thun-der . . .

Every word in the lead has a distinct purpose that obviously contributes to conveying the idea. The lead has no "fat," it's lean, flashy, and exciting.

Hook the reader in the first few words

In the first example, the reporter opened with the narrow focus of his lead in the first five words: "The cold, gray eyes narrowed . . ."

The reader's attention is immediately attracted. He will probably read further . . . and further . . . and further, until he is deeply immersed in the story.

Many mass communications experts say that if you don't hook the reader in the first few words, you will probably lose him.

A good writer will always begin his lead with a clout.

Among the more obvious signs of amateurism is the tendency to open a sentence with "there were, there are, there will be, or there is." This is perhaps the dullest possible way to begin a sentence, and, invariably, a way exists in which fewer words must be used. To begin a lead with a passive verb is inexcusable.

Still another common example of missing action in the first few words is "backing into the lead." The writer attempts to put the lead material in proper perspective by starting with qualifying words. Examples are:

> A few weeks ago . . .
> In a small town nearby . . .
> Despite great opposition . . .
> A long time ago . . .

The reader must bear with the story for several words before the reporter says anything really interesting. Many readers will simply turn to another story instead.

Are readers really *that* fickle? Newspaper readership surveys invariably show that, when a story "jumps" to another page, most readers turn to another story rather than follow it inside. Since jumps normally come after several inches of copy, the reader who refuses to turn to the inside page was obviously interested in the story when he encountered the fatal words, "continued on page 20."

In summary, the reporter must entice the reader with the lead. Even if the body of the story is outstanding, few readers will wade through a dull lead to reach that exciting story which you worked very hard to research and write.

EXERCISES

1. Assume that you are writing a personal profile story about your instructor. White a descriptive lead that will capture his image and character.
2. Clip one or more feature stories from your local newspaper. Paste them on separate sheets of paper, and, at the top of the sheet, identify the type of lead used. Then write a different type of lead based on information given in the story. You may also analyze the leads in your clipped stories for effectiveness.
3. Use your imagination and write fictitious leads of each type given in this chapter.
4. Write the leads below using information provided:

Summary. Mrs. Pauline McCrory, 87, who receives $470 a month from pensions and social security, was arrested last month for shoplifting a cabbage from the Big Bargain Supermarket. She admitted that she has been shoplifting food for six months so that she would have enough to eat. Inflation has raised her rent, transportation and clothing costs so much that she can't buy enough food to eat.

Narrative. After their pleasure sailboat, The Sea Urchin, sank in the Atlantic Ocean, Richard Davis, 35, his wife Joyce, 33, and their children Dorothy, 13, Lucy, 11, and Michael, 9, clung to the floating, overturned hull for three days, during a storm, before a Coast Guard cutter rescued them from skyscraper sized waves whipped up by a 40 knot wind.

Descriptive. The traditional Alabama-Auburn football game was a sell-out with 72,000 people sitting in Legion Field Stadium in Birmingham. Alabama fans wore wide-brimmed red hats, emblazoned with a large white "A." Auburn fans wore blue and orange hats. Each side of the field seemingly tried to drown out the other side's noise, as each band simultaneously played its school's fight song, while fans screamed their respective cheers of "War Eagle" (Auburn) and "Roll Tide" (Alabama).

Teaser. For the third time this month, police unsuccessfully tried to raid a "boot joint"—an establishment where illegal liquor sales are made and gambling is illegally permitted. Vice detective Joe Lewellen, a former Central High School champion sprinter, explained the failures as resulting from technology. The boot joints station a lookout near the front door—usually the only entrance. When police approach, he presses a buzzer which warns the gamblers and bartender to put away illegal gambling materials and illegal liquor. "Several times, I ran to the back room as fast as I could," Lewellen said. "By the time I got there, a dozen grown men were sitting around a huge craps table, smiling innocently. It just goes to show you that you can't out-run electricity."

Using the information from the "teaser" example, write a question lead, a quotation lead, a direct address lead, and a freak lead.

4 : The Body and Ending

Let's assume you have a lively, attractive lead. Your next problem—and sometimes the most difficult of all—is to arrange your material in a manner that will hold the reader's interest and flow smoothly from beginning to end.

In news writing, the job is somewhat easier because each story is written in the same format: the inverted pyramid. While many feature stories follow a similar form, no iron-clad structure exists for all feature stories. While this makes feature writing more difficult in some respects, it also allows the writer greater flexibility in which he may use his creativity and talent.

An examination of the news story's inverted pyramid reveals that the reason for its use is highly practical.

THE INVERTED PYRAMID

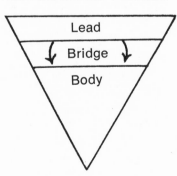

The material is arranged to provide the reader the most important information immediately and, hopefully, to keep his interest. There are two ways of looking at the inverted pyramid:

Material is arranged in descending importance. Information becomes more and more detailed and specific.

In the pressure-packed world of a newsroom, the inverted pyramid accomplishes two other jobs:

It allows the copy desk to chop quickly from the bottom. If the story is submitted seconds before final deadline, the copy desk may not have time to read it carefully. Since the news story is supposedly written in descending order of importance—without an ending—the copy desk can cut from the bottom to make the story conform to available space in the newspaper.

For the same reason, the copy desk knows that the most important aspect of the story should be told in the lead. Thus, when writing headlines under deadline pressure, the copy desk often relies on information in the lead.

What does this have to do with feature structure? The most common form of feature structure is, indeed, an inverted pyramid, but with something extra: an ending.

THE FEATURE PYRAMID

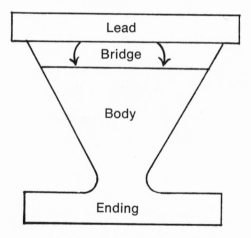

A feature story may—perhaps must—have an ending for two reasons:

1. Because feature stories are often not perishable, there is little reason to hurry the editing process. Instead of having to chop blindly from the bottom, the copy desk may have time to carefully read the story and condense it to meet available space requirements by chopping out words, phrases, sentences and paragraphs throughout the story.

If the story is very well written and exceptionally terse, the news editor may decide to hold the story for a day when ample space is available so that it can be printed with little or no trimming. Feature pages or special magazine supplements are frequently dummied and even printed several days before the particular issue of the newspaper is distributed, so the news editor may be able to plan several days ahead of time.

Even infrequent "deadline" features are edited with special care because the copy desk is well aware that most features have endings, and that feature stories depend heavily on stylish writing that creates reader flow. "Deadline" features are often sidebars—related stories— to major news events.

2. Remember a feature writer is basically a story teller. He carefully arranges his words to effectively communicate his tale. Normally, a story pushes on toward a resolution or a climax. An ending is not only appropriate, but absolutely necessary for many features.

Let's examine a few types of endings.

The Summary Ending. The summary simply ties up the loose ends of the story and points back to the lead. "And they lived happily ever after."

The Stinger. A startling, surprising ending that jolts the reader. The writer simply uses the body of the story to set up the reader for the unexpected conclusion. The stinger ending is a close cousin to the modern movie trend in which the "good guy" loses out to the "guys in black hats."

The Climax. This ending is popular in stories written in chronological order. It's closely akin to the traditional literary format except that, in the feature story, the writer stops at the point where the outcome of the story is clear, rather than continuing in literary form through a post-climax wrap-up.

The un-ending. The writer purposefully ends by emphasizing a key, unanswered question. The reader isn't sure whether the protagonist wins or loses. He wraps up the story just before the climax, either because the outcome isn't yet known or because the writer simply wants to leave his readers hanging.

EXAMPLES OF FEATURE ENDINGS

Summary. A feature story on the last day of the annual state fair, which tried to capture the human side of the fair and reactions to the myriad activities, may end in a summary:

> Clutching a red and white teddy bear under her arm, Cindy Lewis 9, gazed longingly back at the bright lights of the midway and asked her mother, "Can we come back next year?"

Stinger. A feature story dealing with the careful, painstaking training of a race horse may build steadily toward the big race. The readers have been carefully convinced that victory is at hand: the months of preparation are leading to a successful climax. Then the writer uses a stinger ending:

> But as the starting gates snapped open and the thundering hooves of seven glistening thoroughbreds churned the moist track, number 4 faltered and fell behind.
> And, as the jockies urged their steeds across the finish line, mighty "Bright Starlight" had finished dead last.

Climax. Using the same example, a happier climax could make a natural ending. Let's pick up after "Bright starlight" falters.

> But, as the horses entered the stretch, "Bright Starlight" slowly closed the gap. With long, stretching strides, she was suddenly beside the leader as the finish line loomed ahead.
> At the finish line "Bright Starlight" and "Coal Smoke" appeared absolutely tied. But when the film from the photo-finish camera was developed, "Bright Starlight's" nose was a fraction ahead to win.

Un-ending. Again, using the same example, the writer decides to end his feature on a suspenseful note:

> As the starting gates snapped open and seven thundering thoroughbreds churned the track, "Bright Starlight" glistened with sweat as she strode after the goal she had been trained to win.

The endings, in each case, are natural. They fit the story which the writer was trying to convey.

A writer should carefully assess his endings to make sure that they are logical conclusions to his story. Often, when a writer feels that the ending is weak or unnatural, he has only to look a few paragraphs higher in the story to find the perfect, logical ending. The common tendency is for the writer to become so immersed in his story that he continues well past the natural conclusion.

The feature ending is actually one of the easier elements to write. Student journalists often bungle endings simply by trying too hard and, thus, ignore the obvious. Revert back to the "old story teller" role and, rather than seek that fantastic combination of just-right words, simply let the story end itself—naturally. Then, after the ending is apparent, you may, indeed, search for the just-right way of expressing the conclusion.

As you may perceive from some of the endings, the common "inverted pyramid" feature structure may not be applicable to some stories. If the story is more interesting if related in sequential order, you may want to use a chronological pyramid:

CHRONOLOGICAL PYRAMID

```
┌─────────────────────────────┐
│           Lead              │
└─────────────────────────────┘
          Bridge

           Body


┌─────────────────────────────┐
│          Ending             │
└─────────────────────────────┘
```

After a strong lead and a brief bridge, the writer simply relates the story as it happened, building to a climax, a stinger, or even an un-ending.

This format is especially useful in relating adventures, unusual chains of events, or in writing "brights"—short, concise features about humorous or unusual vignettes.

> Perhaps it was a sign of the times, but any sailor who passed by the U.S. Post Office this morning may have had a chuckle.
> At 7 A.M., postal clerk Joe White sleepily walked up to the flagpole, fastened Old Glory to snaps on the rope, and hoisted her up to full mast.
> An hour later, White hastily trotted back to the flagpole and gazed in embarrassment: the flag was flying upside down.
> "I guess I was a little sleepy this morning," White said, chuckling. "I knew something was wrong when the Navy recruiter phoned and asked if the Post Office was sinking. An upside-down flag means ship in distress."

As in the case of leads and endings, the professional journalist knows that the format of the body must be natural. He cannot force a story to fit the inverted pyramid when the story really lends itself to a chronological pyramid or, in some cases, no pyramid at all.

Longer features may require a mixture of formats. The feature may be written basically in the inverted pyramid, but, within that pyramid, a long chronological sequence fits naturally.

Regardless of the reporter's personal preference for structure, the professional will always strive to tell the story smoothly, logically and naturally, using whatever structure—or lack of structure—may be required to do the job of story telling.

TRANSITIONS

You are writing a feature story based on lengthy notes that cover diverse facts about your subject. Each bit of information is like a brick which must be added to another brick to build your story. Between the "bricks" of material are transitions—the mortar that holds the story together.

Transitions may be single words, phrases, sentences or even paragraphs. They accomplish two vital jobs:

1. They inform the reader that you are shifting to new material.
2. They put the new material in proper perspective.

Common examples are: Later; nearby; a few miles away; however; but; an opposition spokesman denied the charge; in other developments . . .

In hard news stories, transitions are easy to find. The writer compresses facts into a crisp, logical rendition of facts that utilizes little stylish writing.

Shotgun-waving masked bandits robbed the Capitol City National Bank of $400,000 this morning.

The bandits burst through the front door at 9:15 A.M., ordered customers and employees to lie face-down on the floor, then cleaned out cash drawers and safe deposit boxes.

During the robbery, a shot was fired, but no one was injured.

According to witnesses, the robbers fled in a 1969 white Volkswagen stationwagon.

Later, police sergeant William Bowling found the get-away car abandoned a mile from the bank. No trace of the money was found.

Near the abandoned car, police found empty money bags with the bank's trademark imprinted on them.

Before the robbery, police were alerted by federal bureau of investigation agents that three out-of-state bank robbers were thought to be in the city.

However, an F.B.I. spokesman said the three robbers, who appeared to be in their mid-20s, do not match descriptions of the three out-of-state men.

The transitions are underlined to help you identify them. In each case, the transition is concise, unobtrusive, and utilitarian. The reader is forewarned that new material is coming, and he is informed of the perspective with which to view the material.

Conciseness and subtleness are desired virtues for transitions. The reader shouldn't be consciously aware of them—the transition shouldn't become an obstacle.

Think of a transition as a "stop" sign. If, instead of "stop," the sign said, "please decelerate completely and place your foot on the brake pedal and press down until your vehicle becomes immobile," the driver would be well into the intersection—and possibly en route to the hospital—by the time he perceived the message. *Be concise.*

If the stop sign were too obtrusive—perhaps a 40-foot flashing neon sign—the driver would be so startled and distracted that he would miss the basic message: Stop. *Be subtle.*

In feature writing, transitions tend to be longer but less frequent than in news stories. Each block of material is developed more fully in feature stories, thus eliminating the need for transitions for several paragraphs. Yet, when a feature writer shifts into a new area, he may need more words to do the job.

A personal profile story, for example, may require several paragraphs of lead-in material to establish the nature and character of the subject. When new material is introduced—often designed to show different perspectives of the subject—transitions such as these are used:

Despite such praise, opponents take a different view . . .

His eventual rise to political power may be rooted in childhood dreams.

To escape the mounting pressures of his office, Smith turns to outdoor sports each Saturday morning.

In these examples, transitions took the form of paragraphs and long phrases, rather than the single-word form used in news stories.

WRITING TECHNIQUES

The skeleton of the feature story is now complete: the lead is the skull, the structure is the backbone, the ending is the tail, and transitions are the ligaments that hold it all together.

In fleshing out this strange beast with interesting material, the writer must use a technique to keep everything in place, serving as the skin. Although there are many such writing techniques, three basic ones are:

Spiraling. Each paragraph elaborates on an item from the preceding paragraph.

Block Paragraphing. Material is presented in separate, complete blocks of material. Note: if the paragraph becomes too long, arbitrarily break it into several smaller paragraphs.

Theming. Each paragraph underlines or restates the lead.

Actually, most professionals alternate several techniques in a given story, depending on length and the nature of the material. This is done to break the monotony that comes from over-use of any one technique.

In writing, several basic guidelines are used to present the material in the most attractive manner possible to lure readers:

Short Paragraphs. A long paragraph, when set in type, can become vicious, menacing monster. It scares readers away because the story appears to be hard to read. Arbitrarily break off a paragraph when it seems to be getting too long. Two rules of thumb are: break off when you approach four typewritten lines; or write only one sentence to a paragraph.

The former rule is perhaps more effective because, at times, two short sentences make a natural—and reasonably short—paragraph. Also, human nature may instigate the creation of the longest sentences in the history of mankind.

Please note that you are writing in journalistic style, not formal English. While English teachers stress the importance of grouping all related material—a complete thought—in a paragraph in formal essay writing, the practical journalist quickly sacrifices form for the ability to communicate.

Write in short, simple sentences. Long, highly complex sentences may, on occasion, be grammatically correct. Yet, if the reader is lost at some insidious turn somewhere between the verb and the object, the writer has failed to communicate. But do not become a short sentence fanatic. If each sentence takes the subject-verb-object form, readers will be hummed into drowsiness within two paragraphs.

The trick is to make sure that each sentence is easy to follow and easy to understand. In many cases, a simple sentence will do the job effectively. But, a total dedication to simple sentences is boring, choppy and sophomoric.

Still another reason for simple sentence use is that complex sentences greatly increase the risk of those pesky hanging modifiers. Although, in journalism, some basic rules of formal English are bent somewhat, grammar must be technically correct.

SUMMARY

Now that you have the basic tools with which to write a feature story, let's construct a feature from scratch, examining techniques, and elements:

As police reporter, you overhear two officers talking about an elderly woman who sweeps the sidewalk in front of her house at 2 A.M. each day. The officers tell you that she not only sweeps the segment running past her property, but sweeps it the length of the block. Curious, you join the officers on their patrol the next night in hopes of seeing the women.

At exactly 2 A.M. the officers cruise down Davis Drive and, sure enough, you see an elderly woman sweeping. The policeman stop the cruiser and greet the woman who smiles back. You approach her, and identify yourself as a newspaper reporter. After an initial exchange of greetings you say, tactfully:

"It's great to see someone with community pride, but why do you do the sweeping at 2 A.M. each day?"

"I don't want the neighbors to see me and think I'm trying to be a do-gooder. The sidewalk gets filthy and the city doesn't clean it, so someone should," she replied.

Now, you know you have a feature story, so you get down to business.

"Will you please tell me your name, and where you live? I would like to do a story about you," you tell her.

"Story? I don't want this in the paper, I don't want my neighbors to know. Why do you think I'm out here at 2 A.M.?"

"I realize that," you say. "But I hope you'll reconsider because this community needs to develop such spirit, and you would make a great example. Maybe more people will start taking pride in their property and doing things for the community. Also, when the city fathers read this, they made decide to start cleaning sidewalks."

The woman ponders your argument, hesitates, then agrees.

"If you really think it would help . . ."

"Definitely," you reply.

"My name is Sandra Strobel and I live over there at 1611 Davis Drive," she said.

"How old are you? How long have you been doing this?"

"I'm 72 years old—I'll be 73 in two weeks—and I've been doing this since George, my husband, passed away last year, a year ago. I don't really have much else to do and all my neighbors are busy, always working, so this is just my little part."

"Other than these police officers, has anyone ever stopped to talk to you?"

"Not many people are up and around this early," she said, chuckling. "Sometimes kids drive past on Sunday mornings. They honk their horns and yell, 'put your back into it, Grandma.' It doesn't bother me, they're just kidding me. They always wave.

"One time there was a burglar. These officers know about it. Anyway, I went outside to do my sweeping and I saw this young man sneaking around the bushes. So, I tip-toed back in and called police. These two fine officers came just two minutes later and caught him trying to crawl into the window next door."

The officers nodded and grinned.

"Does the sidewalk really get that dirty each day?"

"No," she admitted, "It doesn't get that dirty, but an old woman like me needs some reason for being on God's earth. With George being gone and all the children and grandchildren grown up, this gives me something to do, something to look forward to."

"Are you ever worried about your safety?"

"No, not with my police friends around. These two boys make a point of cruising by every night to make sure the crazy old lady is safe. It takes me a half hour to sweep the sidewalk and they always come at 2:10 and cruise back by at 2:20, just like clockwork."

The officers grin sheepishly. "She's a nice lady, so, if we're not tied up, it's a good time to make our check of this neighborhood," Patrolman Wally Brown said. "I didn't know we were that obvious."

"Do you like your neighbors?"

"They're just wonderful to me," she said. "The children call me Grandma and come to visit me all the time. I bake them cakes and cookies if their mothers don't mind. The men are so nice about helping me lift things and fixing things for me. They even painted my house last month for nothing. And the women, I was pretty sick last January and they took turns taking care of me. Not many old women are as lucky as I am. If it weren't for my neighbors, I'd be in an old folks home."

With a merry laugh, she added, "I might be old, but I try to think young. That's what makes life interesting, thinking young. I wouldn't last a month in an old folks home because there aren't any young people there to enjoy."

You thank her for the interview and return to the police car. You sit and watch her for a moment. She bends forward slightly over the well-worn broom and swishes it slowly but rhythmically, whistling a spirited church hymn softly. Her walk is the wobbly, cautious step of an elderly person. Her snow-white hair is tightly arranged in a bun. You recall that she has dark brown eyes that twinkle with merriment, belying the deep wrinkles of age that cover her face. The winkles tell a story of jollyness because they form patterns around her eyes and mouth that come from 72 years of smiles.

You have material for a first rate feature. In the fashion of a good reporter, you used tact and personality to persuade the woman to talk to you. Recognizing human nature, you played on her community spirit to give her a good reason for allowing the story. While other questions could be asked which could produce even more good material, you recognize that you have all the elements you need. The next step is writing the story:

Selecting the Lead. Glancing at available material, you see that your story could lend itself to descriptive lead, a summary lead, a quotation lead, or a narrative lead. Other leads are also possible, but you decide that the material is better suited for those leads. Because of personal preference, you decide on either a descriptive lead—your favorite—or a narrative.

You try a descriptive lead first:

> Only a bright street light and the steady whisking of a battered broom break the 2 A.M. silent darkness that masks Davis Drive when the old woman begins her nightly task of cleaning the sidewalk.

In this *descriptive lead,* the setting receives primary focus to emphasize the unusual circumstances. After establishing the setting, the writer tickles the readers' curiosity by shifting the focus to the old woman and her sweeping chore.

> Mrs. Sandra Strobel, 72, has swept the block-long stretch of sidewalk in front of her 1611 Davis Drive house at 2 A.M. almost every night—health permitting—for about a year.

The *bridge* simply answers the most obvious questions raised by the lead.

A *summary lead* is simpler, and, with a very strong feature subject, it is effective:

> At 2 A.M. each morning, Mrs. Sandra Strobel, 72, sweeps the block-long stretch of sidewalk in front of her 1611 Davis Drive House.

The use of the *time element*, in this case, doesn't constitute "backing into the lead" because the time element is unusual and eye-catching.

A *narrative lead* is moderately effective, but it lacks the strong element of action which is needed:

> Hobbling along the sidewalk at 2 A.M., the old woman busily sweeps along the 1600 block of Davis Drive, whistling a joyous church hymn.

You select the decsriptive lead and continue after the bridge:

> "I've been doing this since George, my husband, passed away last year," Mrs. Strobel explained with a friendly smile. "I don't really have much else to do. All my neighbors are busy, always working, so this is just my little part."
>
> The serenity of the nightly task is broken only by the regular passing of a police car. Patrolmen Richard Evans and Wally Brown manage to patrol the street when Mrs. Strobel is out.
>
> "She's a nice lady, so, if we're not tied up, it's a good time to make our check of this neighborhood," Brown said.
>
> "These two boys make a point of cruising by every night to make sure the crazy old lady is safe," Mrs. Strobel said merrily. Despite her self-repreciating descriptions as "a crazy old lady," Mrs. Strobel expresses the philosophy of a realist.
>
> Admitting that the sidewalk doesn't accumulate very much dirt in a day, she explained, "an old woman like me needs some reason for being on God's earth. With George being gone and all the children and grandchildren all grown up, this gives me something to do, something to look forward to."
>
> At first, she was reluctant to talk about her nightly attack on sidewalk dirt. Her neighbors aren't aware of her task.
>
> "I don't want the neighbors to see me and think I'm trying to be a do-gooder. The sidewalk gets filthy and the city doesn't clean it, so someone should," she said. "I don't want this in the paper, I don't want my neighbors to know. Why do you think I'm out here at 2 A.M.?"
>
> Only an appeal to her civic pride convinced her to tell her story in hopes that other citizens would follow suit—but during daylight hours.
>
> At 2 A.M., the streets are deserted, except for an occasional carload of partying youths, she said.
>
> "Not many people are up and around this early," she said, chuckling. "Sometimes kids drive past on Sunday morning. They honk their horns and yell, 'put your back into it, Grandma.' It doesn't bother me, they're just kidding me. They always wave."

Her nightly vigil has, on at least one occasion, served as a crime deterrent in protecting sleeping neighbors.

While sweeping, Mrs. Strobel saw a young man "sneaking around the bushes. So I tip-toed back in and called police. These two fine officers came just two minutes later and caught him trying to crawl in the window next door."

During daylight hours, the people next door and all along the block call Mrs. Strobel "Grandma." Her wizened eyes soften with affection as she talks about her neighbors.

"They're just wonderful to me," she said. "The children call me Grandma and come to visit me all the time. I bake them cakes and cookies if their mothers don't mind. Everyone calls me Grandma. The men are so nice about helping me lift things and fixing things for me. They even painted my house last month for nothing."

As for neighborhood women, they cared for Mrs. Strobel during a bout of illness last January, she said.

"Not many old women are as lucky as I am," she said. "If it weren't for my neighbors, I'd be in an old folks home.

"I might be old, but I try to think young. That's what makes life interesting, thinking young.

"I wouldn't last a month in an old folks home because there aren't any young folks to enjoy."

After the interview, you contacted several neighbors to get material for this natural and effective ending:

Neighbors along the block said that the affection is mutual.

"Grandma is the most wonderful thing this neighborhood has," Mrs. Brenda Fowler, her next-door neighbor, said later. "We all love her dearly."

Despite Mrs. Strobel's efforts to hide her "do-gooder" 2 A.M. task, neighbors have known all along.

"We just didn't have the heart to let her know," Mrs. Fowler said. "It would have ruined her joy at giving us her special gift."

EXERCISES

Divide the street sweeper story into two parts, research and writing, and examine each carefully.

1. *Research:*

The story subject, Mrs. Strobel, was initially reluctant to talk to the reporter. The reporter recognized basic human nature and provided her with an excuse to overcome modesty on the premise of civic pride. How would you approach her? Are there other ways?

Reporters frequently see questions they could have asked to gain more information after returning to the office. These missed questions result in informational "holes" in the story. Do you see any unasked questions which could have provided important information?

The reporter eventually selected a descriptive lead. Which lead would you have selected? Can you write a better one?

Examine the story structure closely. Does it follow the feature inverted pyramid with ending? Does it really have a structure? What writing techniques are used? (spiraling, etc.)

2. *Writing:*

Retype the story, leaving sufficient room between lines for editing. Underline transitions. Read each sentence carefully and look for ways of saying the same thing in a more concise and effective manner. Make corrections.

On a separate piece of paper, write your own version of the story from the raw information collected by the reporter.

Examine the ending. What kind of ending is used? Is it natural, or is there a better one? Discuss.

5 Tools of Good Feature Writing

Now that you have the basics, let's wheel out the heavy artillery that a professional newsman uses to conquer reluctant readers: *focus, description, anecdotes* and *quotations*.

In the previous chapter, you saw these elements at work even if you didn't really recognize them. The reporter adhered religiously to the basic story he had to tell, thus achieving focus. He concocted a mental image of Mrs. Strobel for the readers to see, thus using description. He carefully sprinkled small stories of Mrs. Strobel's experiences over the year throughout the feature—such as the would-be burglar—to use anecdotes. And he quoted heavily, thus allowing Mrs. Strobel to add flavor to the story by using her own words when effective and appropriate.

Let's examine these basic story-telling techniques:

FOCUS

Focus is a key step in both selecting the story topic and writing the story. Think of focus as being a builder's plumbline. By settling on a narrow, manageable story topic, the plumb line is clearly and truly laid out. In writing the story, each bit of information must touch that plumb line. If the plumb line is not perfectly vertical, the building will be a leaning tower of Pisa. If the craftsman (reporter) doesn't carefully center each brick—story element—on the plumbline, it will collapse.

ILLUSTRATION OF FOCUS

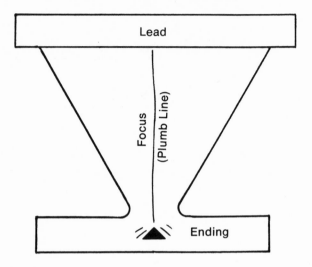

In selecting the topic, the reporter must be very careful to choose an approach that is narrow enough to manage yet broad enough to provide sufficient interesting material.

A reporter may be assigned to write a feature story on changing men's hairstyles. If the reporter attempts a story on the overall, broad topic, he would find enough highly relevant material to write a novel of *War and Peace* proportions. Yet, if he narrowed the subject to the technique used in giving a razor cut, the reader would be bored with inane detail.

Instead, the reporter may consider dozens of story "angles" which are both manageable and interesting.

1. He may seek an old, neighborhood barbershop and chat with barbers who have been shaping hairstyles for years. The angle would be a look at changing hairstyles through the eyes of a couple of barbers. The viewpoint would be strong and amusing.

2. He may visit one of the newfangled men's hairstylist shops, talk to a hairstylist about the "in" styles, and to customers about why they come to a hairstylist.

3. He may seek the women's point of view on whether new styles really improve masculine attractiveness, or whether they prefer the shorter hair of yesteryear. While any such article would be "unscientific" in representing views of all or even most women, it could be effective if coupled with a lighthearted writing approach and an interesting group of women to survey—say fashion models, airline

stewardesses, or other groups of young women who are in "glamour professions."

While these viewpoints—angles—are diverse, they have one thing in common: focus. In each case, the writer has a strong story theme and plentiful material on which to draw.

Focus is also applicable in writing the story. In the above example, the writer many have to fight off temptation to drift into material on clothing styles, favorite dating entertainment of modern couples, or any of hundreds of loosely related areas.

The danger in submitting to the temptation is that the unrelated material will confuse or bore readers and interrupt the flow of the story. When the writer drifts off the "plumb line" of strict adherence to focus, the effect is that both the writer and the readers become lost in a forest of words without purpose, direction or real meaning.

Discipline is the weapon a writer must use to stick to the subject. To be effective, he must be the master of his words and ideas, and not the slave of impulsiveness. While this may seem elementary, even veteran newsmen sometimes slip into digressions that destroy otherwise good features.

Discipline is a combination of attitude and awareness. In attitude, the reporter must totally commit himself to the basic job of communicating effectively with the reader. He must never lapse into the trap of writing to please himself, rather than writing for the people who buy the newspaper. In awareness, the writer must be constantly alert for subtle traps. Even the most conscientious reporter may drift off story focus unknowingly.

To guard against such traps, the writer must question each block of material to be used, before and after the story is written.

Look at your story notes. Examine each bit of information for relevance to the story theme. If it's not relevant or if it does nothing to help you achieve your basic goal of telling that story effectively, cross it out of your notes so that you won't accidently use the material. Be ruthless: if the material isn't clearly relevant, cross it out.

After you have finished writing the story, examine each block of material that you used. Is it relevant to the focus of the story? Does it, indeed, add something worthwhile to your effort of telling that basic story? If not, delete that material because it is detracting from the effectiveness of your writing.

Focus is especially essential in longer stories. When you must handle a great deal of material in providing in-depth coverage of a subject, the chance of irrelevant or unnecessary material is greatly increased.

Simultaneously, the need for weeding out such irrelevancies is also much greater. The length, itself, is a stumbling block to many readers. Remember, you are competing for the reader's time and attention. He may take one look at a very long story and decide that he doesn't really want to devote that much time to the story. Thus, with that in mind, the reporter can make the story more attractive, to a degree, simply by making it a bit shorter through editing out irrelevancies.

Assuming that the reader is interested enough in the subject to start reading it, the next obstacle is to keep that interest so that he will read all of the story you worked so hard to research and write.

Let's say that a third of the way through the story, you lose focus by inserting a block of irrelevant material. After muttering a question concerning the purpose of the material, the reader, who has momentarily lost his reading flow, may quickly take the opportunity to skip to another story.

If the reader skips after reading a third of the material, then the reporter did two-thirds of his work for nothing. Moreover, the newspaper has devoted many column inches of valuable space to copy which isn't read. In short, no one benefits.

To summarize the need for focus, a reporter should:

1. Carefully select his story "angle" so that he can easily manage material necessary to tell the story.

2. Religiously stick to that story angle by eliminating any material that doesn't directly relate to that angle and/or doesn't further the basic goal of telling the story he set out to tell.

DESCRIPTION

In some respects, television has a distinct advantage over newspapers in that the physical description of the person or subject is vividly apparent on the screen. The viewer can instantly perceive and evaluate the subject on television, while a newspaper reader must formulate an image from words in print or, at best, a single photograph showing in an instant the subject from only one angle.

Yet, in other respects, a good writer can turn this disadvantage into a sometimes profound advantage through skillful descriptive writing. The image captured by a camera is superficial and one-dimensional. A weakness of television news media is that time is so valuable that television reporters can rarely go beyond that superficial image. And, even if time is allotted for a half-hour documentary, the inhibiting presence of television cameras may greatly detract from a natural, realistic portrayal.

While a television camera can capture facial features at a given instant, a skillful feature writer can capture *prevailing* features, and the countenance of a public figure when the camera lights are off. More important, a feature writer can describe mannerism, style and idiosyncrasies and, using the skills of a trained observer, emphasize the revealing but often subtle characteristics that give insight to character and personality.

In short, instead of giving the public a one-dimensional picture, the feature writer captures the personality as well as the image. Or, in the case of "things" such as the aftermath of a disaster or a joyful crowd event, the writer can capture the mood.

Good descriptive feature writing is a combination of skills: reportorial news gathering, the highly tuned observation abilities of a newsman, a knowledge of human nature that comes with reporting experience, and the fine ability to put words together in a terse but highly effective manner. With the obvious need for reporting skills, it is little wonder that few if any first-rate feature writers attained their success without a strong apprenticeship in reporting news.

In gathering material for description, a reporter may spend hours, days or even weeks with the subject, carefully observing the countless little things that, when combined, create a strong, realistic image which readers can grasp.

The so-called "new journalism" places great value on this lengthy contact method. In researching for a profile feature on singer Frank Sinatra for *Esquire* magazine, writer Gay Talese spent many days following Sinatra around, noting how he interacted with other people. The result was a highly acclaimed story which is one of the best examples of "new journalism."

During the image-gathering stage, the subject often becomes unaware of the reporter who wisely tries to blend into the woodwork. Hour by hour, the public "front" will flake away, revealing the real person who has never before been portrayed for the public.

Let's take a city councilman, for example. Most politicians tend to be ever-conscious of their public image. They naturally want voters to see them in the most favorable light. Thus, when a television camera is turned on, they may assume a public role that is very different from the private role.

City Councilman John McIntosh is a role-player. To the public, McIntosh is an angry-looking man who quickly assumes a scowl for cameras to underline his image as the angry defender of the common citizen. Almost invariably, McIntosh votes "No" on any given bill.

Yet, through the "eye" of the camera, citizens cannot know that McIntosh is actually a jovial, amiable man who candidly admits his role-playing. A feature writer, using descriptive techniques, can effectively portray McIntosh by emphasizing the public versus private image angle.

The same advantage is available to a writer in portraying an event. A very real "people story" may literally be right under the nose of the television cameraman—and totally inaccessible to him.

At a World Series baseball game, hundreds of sportswriters, broadcasters and cameramen gather to give tedious details of every pitch thrown in the game. Yet beneath the battery of television cameras sit thousands of people who are experiencing a highlight of their lives. And, in cities and towns across the nation, there are millions of people who would like to be sitting in the ballpark to enjoy the "color" as well as the action.

Many newspapers send feature writers to such events to write "color stories." The feature writer ignores the game—at least professionally—and concentrates on capturing the mood and the feeling of that strange beast called a crowd. While sportswriters note whether the pitcher threw a curve or a slider to strike out the cleanup hitter, the feature writer talks to children, grandmothers, hotdog vendors, and "plain ole fans" to capture the crowd color and the many, many viewpoints of the same event. He may stand on the homeplate after the game, slowly turning to get the player's view of the crowd. He may talk to ticket scalpers before the game and players' wives afterwards.

The end result is a story which puts the reader in a choice seat behind third base and allows him to see, hear and even smell the things that fans paid $10 to see, hear and smell at the stadium.

The you-are-there effect is vital to effective feature writing, and it can only be achieved through description.

A feature story on narcotics detectives can be lifted from a run-of-the-mill status to that of a first-rate experience for readers through the skillful description of expressions on the faces of arrested suspects and the subtle signs of nervousness which the officers may well display prior to a dangerous raid.

In summary, descriptive writing is the flesh that fits over the skeleton of the story to make it a living, breathing entity that will captivate readers' interest and give them a far more realistic perspective than they could otherwise gain.

The techniques of descriptive writing are varied and individualistic among reporters. With experience, most reporters develop their own techniques of gathering descriptive material and weaving it into their stories. Yet, for learning purposes, here are some suggestions:

Guidelines for Descriptive Writing

1. Remember that you are, in effect, the eyes, ears and nose of your readers. Your job is to gather an assortment of material which the readers can analyze and assimilate into an image. In this role, always be aware of any characteristic, however subtle, that would aid readers in coming up with an accurate image.

2. Don't allow your presence as a reporter to influence the subject. Try to blend with the woodwork so that you can observe the subject in a natural state. When it's necessary to conduct an interview, try to put the subject at ease so that he will act more naturally.

3. Gather an abundance of notes—much more than you can use. Then, before writing, sift through your notes to determine which observations most effectively capture the whole subject.

4. In writing, spread description throughout the story. Large "glumps" of description may get in the way of reader flow.

5. A fine line exists between the presence of too much description and the absence of too much description. That fine line is the feature writer's target. If the story is tedious with descriptive detail, chop lesser important details. If the story doesn't succeed in allowing you to "see" the subject, add more description.

6. Although a writer should, indeed, act as the ears, eyes and nose for his readers, he should never try to assume the role of their brain by inserting his personal conclusions and interpretations. Often, such conclusion is only a lazy short-cut for good descriptive writing.

A careless writer may describe a woman as being "pretty." Since "pretty" is a relative term, many readers may disagree if they were to see the subject. Also, with the rise of Women's Liberation Movement, many female readers may be offended by the writer's insensitivity to their viewpoints.

The writer may sidestep such well-founded criticism and write much more effectively by remembering that he isn't the readers' brain.

"Pretty" may be deleted for realistic description such as this:

> Her large brown eyes peeked from beneath blonde bangs, twinkling with humor. She wears no makeup because "I don't have to rely on warpaint to attract men. And, even if I needed it, I wouldn't wear it."

In this technique, the writer used a dash of concrete description to aid readers in conjuring a mental image. Then he established her physical attractiveness ("pretty") and gave readers a touch of insight to her personality by using an effective quotation.

ANECDOTES

The story-telling talents of a feature writer are often stimulated in the acquisition and use of anecdotes—concise accounts of humorous or interesting incidents—which give insight to the story subject while entertaining the reader. In a feature, anecdotes serve as stories-with-a-story; they are tales by or about the subject.

Gathering anecdotes may be more difficult than one would think. A feature writer may talk to dozens of people who know the subject, seeking anecdotes which will provide character insight. The problem is that friends may be very reluctant to relate any story which could show the subject in a less than favorable light.

For example, the author once gathered material for an in-depth feature story on a highly respected black city leader, who had an abundance of friends of all races and social positions.

An interview with a close friend of the subject went like this:

> Interviewer: "I need a few anecdotes about Don—stories about him that will enable me to show readers what he's really like. Can you think of any?"
>
> Friend: (chuckling) "Yeah, I know lots of stories, but let me think about which ones I can tell." (Friend ponders his repertoire of stories with a broad grin, breaking the silence periodically with a chuckle.)
>
> Friend: "Naw, I can't tell those because he would kill me if I did."

The end result was that the friend told several interesting but flattering stories which added life to the feature but gave a one-sided view of the subject.

Dealing with adversaries of the story subject is just as difficult. Anecdotes gleaned from political foes are especially suspect if they are unflattering or damaging. If the stories contain political charges, or tales so unflattering that they could be considered libelous, then the reporter must carefully substantiate the stories.

It should be noted that a feature writer is under no obligation to write a flattering account. He is, instead, obliged to give his readers an accurate portrayal of the subject—blemishes and all—so that they may have sufficient information to make up their minds about the subject.

Beat reporters often collect anecdotes by the bushel during "bull sessions" with people on the beat. Any veteran police reporter can recall scores of police anecdotes that he picked up in the coffee shop, while riding around with uniformed officers, or in off-deadline chats with detectives. A city hall reporter can find a wealth of anecdotes in conversing with politicians and officials.

A reporter's mental storehouse of anecdotes is a vital resource. He can recall them for use in stories about individuals or institutions, or, in some instances, he can write an entire feature story as a collection of anecdotes.

The following is a true collection of anecdotes written as a feature story. With a little imagination, you may see how the separate anecdotes could be used in different stories about individual officers or situations.

A young policeman gazed appreciatively at the bumps and grinds of the stripper at the old Roxy Burlesque House two decades ago, when the now-defunct institution still drew throngs of yokels from outlying counties.

Suddenly, he felt the weight of a friendly hand on his shoulder, turned to see who was there, then dashed across stage with a scream of terror.

The "friendly hand" was a 7-foot boa constrictor that a mischievous snake dancer had quietly placed on his shoulder.

"When I turned around, it hissed in my ear," the now-grizzled sergeant recalled. "The lieutenant just happened to be in the audience, so when I ran across stage, he almost fired me."

As in many police tales, the name of the officer must be withheld to protect the guilty. But, in the rough and tumble world of police work, snakes, painted ladies and terror often give rise to legendary tales that are passed on from generation to generation of policemen.

"Some of our tales are a bit morbid and grizzly, perhaps," Captain Arnold Wilson admitted. "But you must understand that because of the dangers and unpleasantries of police work, we must learn to laugh, to see humor in some strange things, in order to cope with the job."

Another snake recently entered police lore when a young rookie was called to a certain address to assist fellow officers on an unspecified case. The rookie's fear of snakes was well-known.

Arriving at the scene, he approached a group of officers when, suddenly, a huge rattlesnake flew through the air in his direction, amid howls of laughter.

The snake was already dead, but the terrified rookie took no chances. He pulled his service revolver and fired several shots.

The snake didn't move, but the rookie's tormentors did. They leaped into thorny bushes, mudpuddles and rockpiles as bullets ricocheted nearby.

While rookies are prime targets for pranks, sergeants are also vulnerable.

One sergeant had a habit of riding in the backseat of a cruiser to direct two young officers and to catch an occasional nap when things were slow.

A railroad engineer happened to be an acquaintance of one

of his chauffeurs. One night, when the sergeant slept soundly in the bact seat, the young officers pulled onto a railroad track, locked the back doors, and signalled the railroad engineer.

As the powerful beam of the train light flooded the police cruiser, the young officers screamed, "Train, train, get out, get out!"

As the sergeant groggily opened his eyes, the engineer blew the whistle. The young officers howled with laughter as the sergeant desperately fought the locked doors.

Such ingenuity is occasionally applied to police work.

A few years ago, two narcotics detectives used their heads to create a disaster.

They were staking out a suspected narcotics dealer, preparing to move in for arrests, when a woman drug user walked down the street and saw them.

"We knew that she would tip off the suspect, but we didn't have anything to arrest her on," one explained. "So we called her over to the car and took her to the railroad yard. We locked her in a boxcar for safekeeping, then returned to pull the raid. It was a good raid, we made several arrests."

The officers made only one miscalculation. After booking the suspects, they returned to the railroad yard to release the woman.

The train was gone.

"The train went all the way to Cincinnati before she could get off," he recalled. "She was mad as the dickens and she filed a complaint against us. We got into a heap of trouble."

Vice squad officers are known for an age-old initiation rite for unwary new members of their squad. The still-used rites may have begun years ago when Captain Wilson was the latest addition to the squad.

"We knew that a hotel bell-boy ran a ring of prostitutes in a downtown hotel, so I dressed up like a country bumpkin and checked in. My partner was in the lobby, and he was supposed to pretend to be waiting on someone.

"The bellboy offered the 'extra-service' and went to fetch a girl. I walked down the stairs and bought a pack of cigarettes to signal my partner. He was supposed to come into the room in 15 minutes to make the arrest. He would have arrested me, too, so that my cover would still be good.

"The girl came to the room and I started stalling. A half hour later, my partner still didn't show, so I had to make the arrest myself. When I took the girl and the bellboy downstairs, my partner was still sitting there.

"He was reading a comic book and laughing."

Besides prostitution, vice detectives are also charged with cleaning up gambling operations, such as "boot joints"—places where illegal liquor sales are combined with illegal craps games.

Boot joints often use elaborate security systems to thwart police raids. Windows are boarded shut, side and rear doors are nailed and barred, and a lookout is posted at the front door, inches away from a buzzer button that warns customers to clear away gambling paraphernalia and liquor.

A few years ago, the vice squad declared war on such an establishment after several violent incidents inside brought it to police attention.

On the first attempt, police tried a frontal assault. They stormed the front door, hoping to catch the lookout off-guard. The lookout, however, pressed the buzzer as three detectives rushed inside.

The first detective fell over a chair. His colleagues fell over him, to the considerable amusement of the customers.

On the second attempt, two undercover officers tried to pose as customers. "Good evening, officers," the lookout said as they entered. He pressed the buzzer, grinning.

On the third attempt, a bold detective crawled into the coal chute to enter the basement where the craps game was played.

Halfway down the chute, he lost his balance and tumbled down, out of control. He landed in a sprawl in the middle of the giant craps table.

In the cool-headed tradition of the city's finest, the detective quickly pulled out his revolver and spoke the familiar words to startled gamblers:

"Don't nobody move, this is a raid."

You may note that in the above example, the writer used a variation of spiraling to connect the anecdotes into a smooth-flowing story. A characteristic of one incident became the tie-in to the next.

It's easy to see why reporters often refer to anecdotes as "gems," and sprinkle them cleverly throughout a story. The principle is the same as in the method used in selling played-out goldmines in the old west: "salt" the mine with a judicious sprinkling of gold nuggets before the customer drops by. The salesmanship method is applicable to feature stories.

QUOTATIONS

The direct quotation is one of the most effective writing tools in the repertoire of tricks. Regardless of how talented a writer may be, a change of pace is needed the break to monotony of anyone's style.

Novelists use dialogue as a means of breaking monotony. After carefully creating a character, the writer seeks to allow the character to "speak" in that peculiar style that fits the character's personality and background.

The use of quotations—dialogue or monologue—to provide a change of pace and to give insight to characters can easily be seen in children's stories.

Let's say you are reading the story of the Three Little Pigs to children. If you read the story in a monotone, the children would probably fall asleep before the wolf blew down the first house.

Instead, most story-readers tend to use voice variations to add eye-widening vitality. The "wolf" has a deep-throated, gravelly growl, which fits his personality. The pigs have giggly, high-pitched voices. Sandwiched between the dialogue, the storyteller reverts to a normal tone.

Although the tone of voice cannot be effectively noted in writing, the choice of words and the style can be used to show personality. Blend this style with the context of the quotation, and the reader can "hear" the quotation in his inner ear.

For the newspaper feature writer, the skillful use of quotations is a vital force in preventing fickle readers from skipping half of a story after style monotony sets in.

Let's take a quotation and build on it:

"Sometimes, I feel like resigning," the mayor said.

This rather routine quotation—structurally—gives the reader interesting information and, perhaps, a glimmer of insight into the mayor's character. Yet the wording is plain and unspectacular. Without the quotation marks, the simple sentence would blend with any writer's style.

Yet the insertion of the first person pronoun "I" injects a personal note that a scrupulous journalist couldn't use outside quotation marks. Also, the direct quotation added a sense of authenticity to the remark and made attribution quite clear. In effect, the quotation does, indeed, break monotony.

By adding a little, the effect is much greater:

"Sometimes, I feel like resigning," the mayor shouted angrily.

Now you have the voice "cue." The reader's inner-ear perks up as his mind "hears" his honor shouting angrily. Yet, you've conveyed essentially the same information.

While quotations can certainly provide many advantages, the writer must be extremely sensitive to ethical considerations. A quotation should be not only a verbatim account of the subject's words, but it must also be given in the context in which the subject was speaking.

To return to the mayor's remark, the word "angrily" hints strongly at some sort of provocation.

If, during the interview, the telephone rang and someone had greatly provoked the mayor, then the writer is obligated to clarify the incident, particularly if the mayor had generally expressed great satisfaction with his job in other parts of the interview.

It should read:

> "Sometimes, I feel like resigning," the mayor shouted angrily as he slammed down the telephone. A citizen had cursed the mayor over the telephone, causing his face to turn bright red. It was the only unfavorable remark the mayor made about his job.

Still another obligation may fall upon the reporter: the ethical considerations of "off the record" remarks. Let's say that during the interview, the mayor inadvertently disclosed his dislike of another council member.

> "Charlie Jones is the most incompetent, lazy councilman I have ever had the honor to work with," he said. Suddenly remembering that such a remark could result in a great political squabble, the mayor quickly added, "But that's off the record."

In this case, the reporter is not obliged to let the mayor off the hook.

If a reporter agrees to accept information "off the record" beforehand, he is ethically bound not to print it. Any post-facto attempt to place information off-the-record is not binding to the reporter unless he generously agrees.

Another quotation problem may lie in the decision of whether to "clean up" a quotation. While a quotation is essentially a verbatim account of what someone said, most reporters "clean up" grammatic errors as an act of human decency.

Few people consistently use absolutely correct grammar in conversational applications. People talk informally, even highly educated people. A mayor may use a double negative; a police chief may slip in an "ain't" or a school board president's verb may not agree with his noun.

Unless a grammatic error has a direct bearing on the story, or unless it is a public issue or part of a public image, then the reporter may correct the error, as long as he doesn't alter the basic message or choice of words.

The logic behind this courtesy is sound. It avoids unwarranted embarrassment to the subject. While conversational misuse of grammar is widely accepted, such errors stand out nakedly in print.

The subject is more likely to be cooperative with the reporter in the future, particularly if he is aware of the courtesy. As a matter of course, however, very few subjects realize that their quotations have been cleaned up.

In some instances, a reporter may choose to leave a quotation untouched. If, for example, a politician openly appeals to the "common folks" by purposely misusing grammar, then the politician may very well resent a reporter's courtesy when it "makes me sound like an English professor."

The choice of whether to extend the courtesy is the reporter's decision. As long as the decision is based on professional circumstances—and not personal likes or dislikes—few people would question the decision.

In writing quotations, many technical problems are encountered. A common writing flaw among new reporters is the tendency either to over-quote or underquote.

In *over-quoting,* the reporter essentially lets the subject write the story for him by simply arranging quotations and inserting transitions.

Even in a hard-news speech story, this technique is rarely acceptable. Very few people use words concisely during a conversation. As a writer, the journalist should be able to say the message more clearly and concisely by paraphrasing it.

Over-quoting also defeats one of the basic virtues of quoting: breaking the monotony of style. By over-quoting, the reporter simply substitutes someone else's style monotony for his own.

Under-quoting is every bit as damaging. Many new reporters are not confident of their ability to take down words verbatim, so they consistently paraphrase. Paraphrasing extensively loses all of the virtues of quoting.

Guidelines for Quotations

In determining whether to quote directly, you may use these guidelines:

1. Is the quotation well-worded, concise and clear? If the answer is no, then you should probably use a paraphrase.

2. Is the message such that a direct quotation would enhance the impact, clarify attribution, or add to the authoritativeness? If so, then you should probably use a direct quotation.

3. Does the story preceding the material in question tend to over-quote or under-quote? If the answer to the first two criteria questions is "maybe," then you should let the third guideline dictate your decision.

Sometimes, the choice is even more difficult when only a small part of a quotation is salvageable, yet that small part is very good. In such cases, it may be best to paraphrase most of the quotation and use a quotation fragment to capture that interesting arrangement of words:

Mayor Brown condemned the Civil Service Commission for its "blundering, darned fool" approach to meeting council guidelines.

On other occasions, an otherwise excellent quotation may be diluted by a digression:

"Because of the uncooperative attitudes of citizens, who keep bugging us all the time about little complaints, such as barking dogs, loud stereos, noisy kids, private quarrels, lost cats, stolen slingshots, noxious odors from plants, and noisy neighbors, I am resigning," said Police Chief Ed Turner.

The chief became too detailed in mid-quotation, so the reporter may choose to use an elipse:

"Because of the uncooperative attitudes of citizens who keep bugging us all the time about little complaints . . . I am resigning," said Police Chief Ed Turner.

You may recall that in earlier chapters, the need for short paragraphs was discussed. Occasionally, a vital, well-worded quotation may require many lines of type to capture. Yet, the conscientious reporter may want to break up the quotation into several paragraphs:

"Our troubles started after I was fired from my job. Our money ran out three weeks later, so we couldn't pay rent. The landlord kicked us out, even though we had never missed a payment before. I tried, then, to get on Welfare, but they ruled that I was ineligible because I wouldn't accept a job across town. I had no choice because I didn't have enough money for bus-fare. So, for the past two weeks, we have been living in our 1957 Ford, getting handouts of food whenever we could," Smith said.

If the writer decided to use the quotation for effect, he must break it into at least two paragraphs. This can be accomplished by not closing the quotation at the end of a paragraph and adding quotation marks at the beginning of the next paragraph:

"Our troubles started after I was fired from my job," Smith said. "Our money ran out three weeks later, so we couldn't pay rent. The landlord kicked us out, even though we had never missed a payment before.
"I tried, then, to get on welfare, but they ruled that I was ineligible because I wouldn't accept a job across town. I had no choice because I didn't have enough money for bus-fare.

"So, for the past two weeks, we have been living in our 1957 Ford, getting handouts of food whenever we could."

You should note that attribution is necessary only in the first paragraph because the quotation continues. In other cases, when a new quotation is given, it must be attributed each time:

"Our troubles started after I was fired from my job," Smith said. "Our money ran out three weeks later, so we couldn't pay rent. The landlord kicked us out even though we had never missed a payment before."

To continue the story after proper checking, the reporter mixes quotes and paraphrases.

John Austin, Smith's supervisor at Green Grocery Store, said Smith was fired after evidence indicated he was stealing canned goods. Smith denied the thefts.

Smith's landlord, Paul Evans, contradicted Smith's allegation that he had always paid rent before. Evans contended that Smith hadn't paid in four months.

"I tried then to get on Welfare, but they ruled that I was ineligible because I wouldn't accept a job across town. I had no choice because I didn't have enough money for bus-fare," Smith said.

Wanda Mayer, Smith's Welfare case-worker, said Smith turned down three jobs, including one in a store seven blocks from Smith's car which is sitting at W. 19th Street and 35th Avenue. The gas tank is empty.

"So, for the past two weeks, we have been living in our 1957 Ford, getting handouts of food whenever we could," Smith said.

At 1901 35th Avenue, Mrs. Abrigail Smith, Smith's mother, lives in a four-bedroom house. Neighbors said that Smith and his wife slip into the house as soon as it's dark and stay there until sunrise.

SUMMARY

Now you have the tools to breathe life into even the most routine feature story.

Application of the tools of description, anecdotes, quotations and focus should improve with practice and experience.

After awhile, a writer develops a "feel" for the proper use of such tools, just as a skilled craftsman develops a special "touch" in using his tools. Your own individual style will evolve, based partly on your personal preference in choosing words and your own formula for mixing description, anecdotes and quotations.

The long-range effect is to develop a style of writing that will draw readers smoothly through the story, and enthrall them with both the material and your skillful style.

EXERCISES

Part One

You are assigned feature coverage of police activities at the Lee County Fair. The Capitol City Police, who have jurisdiction at the fairgrounds, have started a new program aimed at preventing trouble with youth gangs. In past years, violence has marred the fair activities when the gangs, consisting of impoverished youngsters from rough neighborhoods, have started mischief with fair employees that, invariably, resulted in confrontations between the gangs and police.

This year, Capitol City Police are patterning an approach after the successful "Daisy Patrol" concept in Dayton, Ohio. Officers are trained in crowd-control psychology weeks before the fair. Donations from businessmen have been used to purchase hundreds of ride-tickets which police will distribute to the youths. The ticket distribution not only creates better rapport between police and the youths, but it keeps them well-occupied and out of mischief. Your city editor tells you that he wants you to capture the relationship between police and the youths.

Using this situation, discuss these questions:

1. How would you attempt to achieve a narrow, effective story focus? How would you go about gathering information?

2. What sort of anecdotes would you seek? How would you gather them?

3. While ample description is available at any fair, what sort of descriptions would you look for?

4. How would you gather quotations? What kinds of quotations do you need from the available sources?

Part Two

Using your imagination to conceive focus, anecdotes, descriptions and quotations, weave together a fictitious feature story on this event.

6　Finding a Feature Story

On a slow news day, several years ago, a city editor gloomily checked his meager list of stories for the final edition, glanced up at the clock, then stared at an unfortunate young reporter who had caught his attention.

"You have 90 minutes until final deadline," the city editor said. "Go out and find a nice, light, page one feature."

Since the city editor's tone of voice implied the unnerving postscript of "or else," the reporter grabbed his notebook and hurried outside.

Within five minutes, the reporter spotted his feature story: A two-man window-washing team was working from a platform on the 31st floor of a towering building. He stopped at a payphone, called for a photographer, then took the elevator to the 31st floor, rapped on the window, and then interviewed the window-washers.

The story angle: What is it like to work one backward step away from a 31-story plunge?

With a little imagination, finding a feature story is as easy as that. Open your eyes to all of the fascinating things around you and you will see more feature stories than you can write in a lifetime.

A great advantage in being a reporter is that you have a "license" to find out about all those things you've always been curious about. Many reporters are personally shy, until they have a notebook in their hands. Then, the notebook serves as "Linus' blanket" to enable these reticent souls to satisfy their curiosity.

Some students are understandably apprehensive about finding their first feature stories. While most college coursework requires difficult mental gymnastics, feature writing assignments lead students away from the desk and out into the "real world."

Instead of struggling with formulas and thoughts behind closed doors of a dormitory room, a feature writing student is expected to *create* his own problem (the story idea) and to solve that problem by brazenly approaching stangers and asking what may seem to be foolish questions.

The first feature story is somewhat like learning to swim. You must take a deep breath and plunge right in, despite nagging fears that you will sink to the bottom—forever.

And, like beginning swimmers, the beginning feature writer may wonder why he was worried in the first place after an initial success. It's really a matter of self-confidence, and self-confidence must be individually acquired through experience.

Everyday People, Places and Things: Feature Goldmines

As the young reporter in the opening anecdote found, there are good feature stories wherever there are people. Let's take a student-setting and examine feature possibilities.

One alert student journalist found a superb feature story in a dormitory room. She heard that a male student kept a pet, blackwidow spider with the strange name of "Mine." She arranged to interview the student and asked the obvious questions: Why do you keep such an unusual pet? What does it eat? Is it dangerous? How did you catch it? What does your roommate think about it? Why did you name it "Mine"?

The result? The story appeared in several local newspapers under her by-line.

Similar results were achieved by another student who recalled that some friends kept a pet alligator in their apartment. The 2½-foot reptile, his owners, and the student journalist, gained instant fame in local newspapers.

Hobbies also make interesting stories. An enterprising student made dry flies for trout fishing as a hobby and as a business. He sold many dry flies to sporting goods stores to gain pocket money. A student journalist gave him publicity through a well-written feature story.

Human drama is a fertile field for features. A student wrote a poignant feature about his apartment neighbor who overcame long odds to survive cancer. The neighbor bolstered his courage when doctors told him he had little chance to live by digging his own grave and visiting it frequently to meditate.

Unusual skills are abundant on college campuses. A woman student is a champion judo expert. Another woman student traveled with a nationally-famed singing troupe. A male student is an expert mountain climber.

Foreign students often make good feature subjects. What do they think of the United States? How do customs differ? How do they view such American favorites as football, television soap operas, and skiing? Are they homesick?

Faculty members may also make interesting subjects. A biology professor made several ocean dives in experimental diving craft. Another professor was a shipmate of a President when he served in the Navy.

To move away from campus, townspeople can also be interesting, once you get to know them. The proprietor of the favorite off-campus beanery has seen many generations of students pass through, and he can offer many amusing tales about changing—or never-changing—campus life.

A small shop near campus specializes in American Indian jewelry. The owner is an expert in the beautiful artwork performed by skilled Indian craftsmen, and he can provide tales aplenty about his trade.

Life at campus hangouts can be effectively captured in feature stories. How does the manager keep order when his establishment is overflowing with boisterous students?

Sometimes, enterprising students can spot and intercept stories that are only passing through town. A determined student saw a hobo hop down from a passing freight train. After making a U-turn with his car, the student stopped and persuaded the hobo to talk with him about the strange life of a drifter.

A Chicano student wrote a sensitive, informative feature about illegal aliens and the exploitation they encounter.

Unusual jobs have produced a fine harvest of feature stories. Parking meter maids, policemen, a woman student who worked as a state water patrol employee, a jailer, a crop-duster pilot, and a dog catcher have been among many such topics.

All of these stories about everyday people were written by University of Northern Colorado feature writing students. Most of these stories, written for class, were printed in local newspapers.

FEATURES ON NEWS BEATS

On the professional newspaper level, most feature stories are written by the staff work-horses: the beat reporters.

As discussed earlier, beat reporters write features not only for production, but as a means of winning vital news sources. An honest, accurate feature story rarely alienates the subject. A new reporter on a beat may use features as a crutch until he can develop necessary news sources.

Let's look at city hall beat, one of the toughest assignments for a veteran reporter.

As he walks into the maze of offices that characterizes a typical city hall, the veteran reporter who recently inherited the beat may cast his practiced gaze about in search of feature subjects. He will easily find many.

The city council clerk is a powerful city hall figure who is a master of political intrigue and bureaucratic finagling. An honest and dedicated public servant, he is privy to the behind-the-scenes maneuverings of city government. He is a prime feature subject, both because of his accomplishments and character, and because of his value as a potential news source.

A colorful city councilman is also an excellent feature subject. After spending many years in all phases of politics, he has gathered a wealth of political anecdotes about himself and others.

Looking around the bureaucracy, the reporter sees many valuable sources awaiting feature coverage. The crusty, legendary finance director, the personnel director who has negotiated with labor unions for many years (and who is now engaged in crucial negotiations), the controversial civil service director, and the chief city planner, all can be groomed into news sources through feature coverage.

While this approach is somewhat self-serving for the reporter, it can provide an information bonanza for readers who are interested in city government. It gives the reader the opportunity to get to know the decision-makers who will, through their actions, affect the welfare of every citizen.

A related approach for the new beat reporter is to share his learning experience with the readers. A new city hall reporter must learn the intricacies of city finance, labor procedures, hiring practices, street and building maintenance, planning, housing inspection, water and sewerage service, waste collection, budget-making, contract bidding, and the functions of departments and agencies within city government.

This sometimes mind-boggling educational experience for the reporter can be translated into feature stories. While trying to understand the city budget systems, the new city-hall-beat reporter may write a feature story on the bureaucrat who develops the budget. The story would provide a layman's explanation of how the budget system works.

Within a few weeks, the new city hall reporter will have written dozens of sound feature stories and, in the process, he will have gained dozens of vital news sources and a basic personal understanding of key city hall functions.

Other beats may be even more lucrative in producing feature

stories. When he isn't covering crimes and disasters under intense deadline pressures, the always-busy police reporter has more feature subjects available than he can handle in a lifetime.

By the very nature of the beat, the police reporter encounters more human drama in a week than most people ever encounter.

The new police beat reporter may use the same approaches as the new city hall reporter in using feature stories to make news sources, and to learn about functions within the police department.

After writing features about the officers in charge of such functions as homicide investigations, robbery, burglary, vice, the dispatch center, records section, and other key functions, the new police reporter will slowly win the confidence of men who, because of their profession, do not bestow confidence readily.

The police beat reporter will soon find that the more he knows about his beat, the more abundant feature stories become. After writing the "breaking in" features about the officers and their functions, and after informational sources are functioning smoothly, the human drama of policework and crime opens into a bottomless pit of feature stories.

Each victim of crime is a potential feature story: The store owner who has been repeatedly pistol-whipped by robbers; the elderly purse-snatching victim; the parents of a teenage narcotics addict; the family that lost everything to burglars; the newspaper carrier who was beaten and robbed; and the elderly man who was tricked out of his life savings by con artists.

Regardless of how long a reporter covers police, a ride at night in a police cruiser or with narcotics or vice detectives will invariably provide new, exciting stories for his readers.

The functions within a police department are so diverse that a reporter may write interesting function-oriented features long after he has "broken in." A day in a radar-equipped traffic control car on a freeway will leave a nervous reporter with a notebook filled with observations that were shakily jotted as the car swerved through traffic at high speeds to stop a speeder.

After awhile, the police reporter finds contacts and features on the "other side" among criminals. The confessions of a con artist, a burglar's tips to the worried homeowner, a bookie's guide to gambling, and an intimate look at the leader of a violent street gang may thrill —and perhaps educate—readers.

Many police reporters also cover the fire department. This provides a large feature dividend for resourceful news writers, because the fire department offers many stock feature approaches which, although done repeatedly, always seem to interest editors and readers.

A night in a firehouse is an age-old favorite. The reporter simply joins firemen for a night of fitful sleep that is constantly interrupted by shrill alarms, mad scrambling, and rides through the cold night to danger. Riding on a firetruck fulfills childhood ambitions as well as provides good feature stories for wide-eyed reporters.

Retiring firemen may tell stories so vividly that smoke, fire and collapsing walls seem almost tangible. Firefighting is among the most dangerous of all professions, so feature stories about the men who choose this calling are abundant and interesting.

Coverage of features on police beat and city hall beat is only a small taste of the feature lode available to enterprising reporters on all beats. The education beat reporter can always find features in classrooms, the labor reporter can write about often colorful union officials and the human cost of a strike, the courts reporter can choose from flamboyant attorneys, good natured judges, divorce referees, savvy bailiffs, and the drama of acquittal from the viewpoint of the defendant.

Regardless of which reporting specialty you may inherit, feature stories will present an ever-present opportunity to win news sources, educate and inform your readers, and impress your editors with steady, high production.

CREATING A FEATURE SUBJECT

General assignment reporters, who must operate without the advantage of ready-to-pluck feature stories that are available to beat reporters, often resort to ingenuity to conceive feature stories. Sometimes, this ingenuity is coupled with a guinea-pig instinct of donating your own feeble body for an experiment in human behavior.

As noted in a later chapter, the desire to come up with a "different" feature idea at Christmas has driven many reporters to such strange performances as playing department store Santa Claus or even grabbing a shepherd's staff to shiver in a living Nativity scene.

Human reaction to an unusual circumstance is the basic for thousands of feature stories. While the ploy of testing human reactions can take many forms, the resulting story is usually fascinating to readers who can readily identify with the "average citizens" who encounter the zany reporter.

A reporter once pondered the sad state of Thanksgiving. He noticed that Christmas decorations were glittering all around town on the day before Thanksgiving. Slowly, the idea for a search for Thanksgiving dawned on him. If the Greek philosopher Diogenes carried a lamp around, looking for the elusive honest man, the reporter decided that he could carry his notepad around in a quest for a Thanksgiving turkey on "Thanksgiving Eve."

This may sound simple, except for one detail: the reporter was looking for a live turkey downtown, or at least a Thanksgiving turkey decoration. After wandering vainly around town, the reporter entered a department store pet shop. The exchange with a salesday went this way:

Reporter: Do you have any turkeys?

Saleslady: No, have you tried a supermarket?

Reporter: I mean a live turkey.

Saleslady: (Pausing to look at the strange customer) What on earth do you want with a live turkey?

Reporter: This is Thanksgiving Eve, I want to buy a pet turkey for my kids. You know, like an Easter bunny . . .

Saleslady: We don't have any, but can I interest you in a nice, Thanksgiving boa constrictor?

The reporter passed up the snake and identified himself. The saleslady said no one had ever asked for a turkey before.

The same reporter was assigned Christmas feature coverage, so he abandoned Thanksgiving after writing his feature, then tackled the Christmas season. After writing many "stock" Christmas features, he conceived still another "quest," during a conversation with another reporter and his city editor.

The other reporter recalled that organized crime controlled Christmas tree sales in a Texas city in which he had worked as an investigative reporter. The feature writer decided to check out the possibility that the local mob had cornered the market in his city.

His investigative approach was rather faulty, but his instinct for a humorous feature story wasn't. The reporter simply drove around to several Christmas tree lots, walked up to the salesman, and asked:

"Pardon me, but can you tell me if the mob owns this tree lot?"

It takes little imagination to picture the startled responses he received, particularly from lots operated by churches and charities.

After the initial reaction, the reporter identified himself and chatted with salespeople about the peculiarities of Christmas tree lot operations, particularly the strange antics of the customers who shake down tree after tree. Some salesmen explained methods of fire retardation which the reporter included in his story as a service to the readers.

Another reporter grew a beard as the basis for a feature series. The reactions of friends, acquaintances, readers and everyday people on the street to his facial hair gave him a feature installment at each growth stage. When the beard was sufficiently long, he used it for a more serious story. The reporter dressed himself in militant-styled fatigues and managed to purchase several sticks of dynamite. Then, without the dynamite, he bought an airline ticket and attempted to board a plane. He was stopped and carefully searched by a suspicious airport security officer.

Even the most ambitious reporters sometimes draw the line on "guinea pig" stunts when bodily harm may result. A city editor once suggested to two reporters that they stage a fist-fight on the corner of a busy intersection to see how people reacted.

"You don't have to really hit hard," he assured them.

Each reporter, perhaps suspicious of his colleague, declined.

Following Your Curiosity

The role of curiosity in finding good feature topics has been repeatedly underlined, yet its application in a more mundane scale can be easily overlooked. While curiosity about human behavior led to many of the stories discussed earlier, even the smallest twinge of curiosity can lead to a good feature.

One city editor was fascinated by toys, puzzles and games. During his lunch hour, he frequently scanned toy shelves. If he saw an interesting, complex toy or puzzle, he would purchase it and, on returning to the office, place the game on the desk of an unfortunate reporter.

The reporter, then, would have to figure out the toy or puzzle and write a feature story on it. Puzzle parts, nuts and bolts, plastic parts, and large instruction sheets would be strewn randomly about the desk as the veteran reporter futilely struggled with a puzzle that a 10-year-old child could work in minutes.

The story angle for the games was a natural: How many readers have fumbled madly with such toys and games? People are always interested in people.

The student reporter doesn't have to resort to the often bizarre methods of finding a feature story that the exuberant veteran reporter may undertake. The point of this chapter is that feature stories are so plentiful that they may be plucked, at random, without great effort.

In learning to write feature stories, the student journalist has one great advantage: he doesn't have to worry about whether the story has been done recently in his newspaper or his competitor's newspaper. The student journalist isn't driven to strange antics in search of a fresh angle. That comes later, after professional status is reached.

For now, stick with subjects that are close to you and, most of all, interesting to you. Regardless of how strong a feature topic may be, the reporter must be personally curious and interested in the subject if he is to write a lively, professional story. The examples discussed should serve only as guidelines to help you recognize the techniques of finding a feature.

Now it's up to you. Look around, follow your curiosity and let it lead you to a feature story that you will *enjoy* researching and writing.

Choosing the Right Angle

With a feature story idea in hand, your next task is to decide on the most effective approach to use in telling that story. The approach is called the *story angle.*

Perhaps your city editor assigns you the job of providing a feature story on the State Fair. After a few minutes at a fair, a reporter will realize that it is impossible to cover the multitude of events comprehensively, so he must find the best possible approach—story angle—to use in capturing the overall mood and atmosphere of the event.

The reporter must seek middle ground between two extremes: an angle that is so broad that it is impossible to write a thorough, well-structured story. Or an angle that is so narrow that ample material is non-existent.

In covering the fair, the reporter may go through an exercise in logic to choose his angle:

1. What activities and situations are available? Mentally or physically list everything you can think of.

2. Of these activities, which are most important? You will, automatically, narrow your list to perhaps a half dozen key activities.

3. Is there a common thread in most or all of these key activities? Can this "thread" become your angle so that you may logically touch each key activity?

Let's use an example to illustrate this process:

You are the *Capitol City News* reporter who is assigned State Fair coverage. Arriving at the Fair, you quickly compile a list of activities and events from both the Fair schedule and your observations:

FAIR SCHEDULE—Opening Day

10 a.m.—Fair opens with Ribbon Cutting by Gov. John R. Browning

11 a.m.—Greased Pig Contest in Grandstand

11:30 a.m.—Western Barbeque, $2 a plate, at picnic area

12 noon—Judging of Baking Contest at Exhibition Center 3
Judging of Farm Vegetables at Exhibition Center 4

1 p.m.—Magnificent Hoffmans, acrobats, perform in Grandstand

1:30 p.m.—Hog Calling Contest—Livestock Barn 2
Poultry Judging at Livestock Barn 1

2 p.m.—Handicraft Judging at Exhibition Center 1
Elementary School Art Judging at Exhibition Center 1 (balcony)

2:30 p.m.—Singer Brenda Holmes performs at Grandstand ($2 admission)

3 p.m.—Damley Circus Show begins in Bigtop

4 p.m.—4-H Horse Judging begins in Livestock Barn 2

Dog Show Judging begins in Livestock Barn 1 arena

6 p.m.—Second Circus Performance

7 p.m.—Main Grandstand Performance by comedian Charlie Hayes

9 p.m.—The Thrill-Seekers automobile dare-devils perform in Grandstand

11:30 p.m.—Fair Closes

By 10:30 a.m., you are beginning to acquire a feel for the most interesting subject not covered by the fair agenda: *the crowd of people who are attending.* They quickly swarmed all over the fairgrounds as soon as the governor snipped the ribbon to open the gates.

A crowd has personality, and you note that this crowd has a happy, childish personality that derives from the predominance of children who are gleefully tugging parents along.

You watch the people crowd around stands on the Midway as "carneys" colorfully persuade them to try their luck and skill at a variety of games. The concession stands are swamped by people who hungrily eye hotdogs, cornpups, tacos, cotton candy, popcorn and candied apples.

Suddenly, the story angle begins to take shape. Each event is designed to cater to people, to draw a crowd. With this constant in mind, you ponder the question: How do I use people as the "story thread" when there are so many different people with different viewpoints?

Then you have it! You must find someone with an especially interesting viewpoint and show the key events through this person's eyes.

Examining the agenda, you decide to include these events:

Opening ribbon cutting (You caught the governor's remarks)

Greased Pig Contest

Magnificent Hoffmans

Elementary School Art Judging

Damley Circus

Thrill-Seekers

You also plan to visit as many exhibits as possible to try to add atmosphere to your story.

Looking around, you see several children with their mothers and fathers. You began asking the key question:

"Pardon me, I'm a reporter for *The Capitol City News.* Is this the first fair that your child has attended?"

After a dozen negative answers, you find 7-year-old Dorothy Engles who is attending her first fair with her parents, Mr. and Mrs. James Engles of Bay City. Dorothy's parents, after listening to your suggestion, agree to let you join them.

Your angle is found: A child's view of her first fair.

Hooking the Reader

After following the Engles around the fair, gleaning reactions from Dorothy, you return to the newspaper city room to write your account. You know that your first few words will either "hook" the reader or lose him.

While lead possibilities are endless, you decide to try a blurred-action descriptive lead to capture the dazzling sensory effects of the fair at night.

> A swirling rainbow of lights blurred past as the swooshing wind tried to drown out the caliope's "Davey Crockett" tune and dry the tears of terror from the 7-year-old girl's rosy cheeks.
>
> "Ohhh, H-E-L-P, I want off!" Dorothy Engles screamed as she clutched her father's arm. "It's too fast."
>
> It was Dorothy's first roller coaster ride at her first State Fair. And, while she said she enjoyed the fair, she vowed later that it was also her last roller coaster ride.

In Chapter 3, criteria and options of lead writing were fully discussed. This lead accomplishes all vital objectives: it attacts the reader quickly and it sets the stage for the story to follow. The first few words are "grabbers" which should immediately hook the reader.

Dragging Him Through the Story

After the strong lead, you have many readers hooked. Now, you must carefully reel them in by maintaining strong interest.

Strong adherence to the story focus is, in this case, simple. You allow the girl to show you the fair as a tourist guide would lead a group of camera-clutching Westerners through the maze of monuments in Washington, D.C. The story continues after the lead:

> The roller coaster ride was the single bad experience for Dorothy from the moment she eagerly scampered through the main gate after Gov. John Browning snipped the ribbon at 10 a.m. to open the fair with "There's lots of fun waiting inside," until gates closed at 11:30 p.m.

This transitory paragraph sets the stage for Dorothy's Alice-in-Wonderland journey through the fair which you relate in sequential order.

"As soon as we reached the Midway, Dorothy stopped, stood still for a moment, then turned around slowly with her arms stretched upward, "Mrs. Engles said. "She couldn't believe her eyes."

(Note: This is the moment when you joined the Engles.)

"Step right up, folks, and win a Teddy Bear," a squat, bald carney said enticingly. "Pitch a softball into the milk can and you take your pick."

The carney grabbed a ball and tossed it into the small opening with such ease that Dorothy became excited.

"Daddy, daddy, I want a Teddy Bear," she said. "You can do it."

Grinning knowingly, Engles gave the carney two quarters for three balls, judged the distance, then tossed them one at a time. The first ball missed the can while the second and third balls bounced away near the opening.

"I'm hungry," Dorothy said as they walked away. Turning her deep blue eyes on her father, she added, "Can I have a hotdog? And a candied apple?"

"Which do you want?" he asked.

"Both," she replied, shaking her long, blonde locks.

After the hotdog—without a candied apple—the Engels strolled to the Grandstand to see the Greased Pig contest.

About 20 teenage boys wearing coveralls or blue jeans waited for the crate to open. With an angry squeal, a small pig covered with axle grease cautiously trotted from the cage.

Suddenly, all 20 boys converged on the terrified porker who slithered out of a dozen frantic grasps.

The Engles, who own a farm near Bay City, howled breathlessly in delight as the mud-covered lads missed again and again. Finally, Tommy Peterson, 14, of Oakridge, removed his shirt and used it to scoop up the pig. He won the $25 prize offered by the Capitol City JayCees.

"That boy was the only one who was smarter than the pig," Engles said.

After wolfing down a plate of Western Barbecue in the picnic area, Dorothy led her parents to the Grandstand where The Magnificent Hoffmans were performing their aerial acrobatic act.

Craning her neck way back, Dorothy gazed at the four trapeze artists dressed in red, sequined tights, who sailed and tumbled 50 feet overhead.

When Alfredo Hoffman, the star of the act, fell to the safety net in an unsuccessful double somersault, Dorothy screamed, covered her eyes, then spread her fingers so she could peek through.

At 2 p.m., Dorothy and her parents hurried to Exhibition Center 1 to watch the Elementary School Art judging. Dorothy had entered a water color landscape of cows grazing on her father's farm.

"Oh, they're looking at my picture," Dorothy said, breathlessly, as three judges scrutinized the painting and made notes. As they moved on, Mrs. Engles squeezed Dorothy's trembling shoulder to give needed moral support.

The 30 minutes that passed seemed like 30 days to Dorothy, who fidgeted nervously until the judges returned to announce the winners.

"All the paintings were so good that we had a difficult decision," Clifford Moore, the head judge, said. "The first place ribbon goes to Robert Anders of Northridge for his painting, 'Winter scenes.'"

Dorothy's shoulders sagged and she looked up at her mother with misty eyes.

"The second place ribbon goes to Dorothy Engles, of Bay City, for her painting, 'Grazing Land'," the judge then said.

Dorothy clapped her hands together, then hugged her parents jubilantly.

Still clutching the red, second place ribbon, Dorothy then led her parents to the Damley Circus Show in the Bigtop.

As acrobats formed human pyramids, lion tamers cracked whips, elephants reared on hind legs, and horses galloped in a circle, Dorothy's eyes began to dull into a stupor, as she sat quietly.

"Dorothy has seen so many new and exciting things that she's overwhelmed," Mrs. Engles whispered to her husband.

Fatigue was beginning to slow Dorothy down as they strolled to the 4-H horse judging, then toured the livestock barns and 4-H Club exhibits.

After a quick supper of hotdogs and french fries, they went to the Grandstand for a performance by comedian Charlie Hayes, followed by the Thrill Seeker's automobile daredevils.

Dorothy dozed through much of Hayes' performance, while her parents roared with laughter. Propping her head on her father's lap, Dorothy lay immobile until the high-pitched thunder of powerful automobile engines stirred her.

Rubbing her eyes, Dorothy looked up just in time to see Fred Warner drive a car onto a ramp, then leap over two parked cars. She clapped in appreciation.

She held her breath as cars travelled around the track on two side wheels, and cleared ramps two at a time. In the grand finale, two cars approached each other at a high speed, then flew from ramps, passing only a foot or so apart.

The rejuvenated Dorothy wasn't anxious to leave when the public address system announced that the fair was closing for the night.

As she passed through the main gate, she turned around and gazed with dreamy eyes at the darkening spectacle behind her.

"Can we come back next year?" she asked, as her parents smiled and nodded.

SUMMARY

As you can see, the angle was so strong that most readers would be "pushed" through the story, once they were attracted to it.

The use of quotations and anecdotes was carefully applied so that the reader could look forward to these "gems", and so that the monotony of the writer's style was broken.

This underlines a key truism of feature writing: Once the right angle is found, the story will often write itself.

EXERCISES

1. Clip a feature story from your local newspaper and carefully analyze it to determine the story angle, the technique used by the reporter to "hook" the reader, and techniques used to "push" the reader through the story.

2. Analyze the weaknesses in the story. Did the reporter fail to write an adequate lead to "hook" the reader? Did the story bog down?

3. Using the information from the story, rewrite it to improve it. Use a different type of lead, and, if possible, a different story angle.

4. Make a list of 10 feature story ideas on on near campus. Explain why each idea would develop into a good feature story.

5. Take your best idea and list all available sources of information relating to it. Are sources available for each piece of information that you need?

6. Pretend that you have been assigned Christmas feature cover- both uncommon and practical. Explain how you would gather infor- age for your local newspaper. Conceive a list of story ideas which are mation for each story.

7 Polishing a Feature for Print

Pride of authorship is among the greatest, and most common, sins of writing. This is understandable, considering garden-variety human nature. After slaving over a story for several hours, each sentence, word and phrase becomes a treasured work of art to the writer. It is, then, little wonder that reporters have accused copy readers of having tendencies ranging from sadism to incompetence when a glowing bit of prose is chopped from a story.

Yet, a good professional knows that the copy desk often improves a story by deleting verbose, albeit "beautiful," prose.

An age-old journalistic parable has, as its protagonist, a bright-eyed young reporter who asks a grizzly old city editor for the ultimate wisdom: "How can I possibly improve this story? There's nothing wrong with it."

The city editor doesn't even look up from the copy he is reading. He gruffly tells the young reporter, "Pick out the five best phrases you have, the ones that show your best writing, and underline them."

After following the city editor's instructions, the young reporter proudly handed his boss the story.

To the reporter's horror, the city editor then pencilled out each underlined phrase and handed the "gutted" copy back to the reporter, along with the advice: "That's how you improve a story."

While somewhat brutal, the editor's method underlined a bit of valuable advice: *A reporter must write for the reader, and not to please himself.* By succumbing to the temptation to show off his writing ability, a reporter often weakens the story he is trying to tell.

For student journalists, still another message lies in the parable: If you don't edit out verbosity, someone else will. And that "someone else" may not have the same, tender, "feel" for the basic story that the reporter should have. It is both to the advantage of the reader as well as the reporter if the reporter will swallow his pride of authorship and objectively edit his copy.

On the other side of the fence, editors and copy-readers are well aware of the problem of editing a feature. A good copy-reader will make every effort to strengthen—not weaken—a feature story when it must be trimmed to fit allocated space. Yet, the copy-reader isn't a mind-reader, so he may not understand exactly what a reporter is trying to write. If he errs, then the fault is the reporter's, not the copy-reader's.

METHODS OF EDITING FEATURES

With experience, each reporter learns his own method of editing feature stories. The editing techniques which will be discussed below should be altered to fit the individual style of each reporter. The main point is that editing must be systematic and thorough, so that, by following a procedure, the reporter will automatically catch errors, verbosity, reader-flow obstacles, and other problems that detract from good feature writing.

Editing Features Under Deadline Pressure

While *most* features are not written under deadline pressure, some "sidebars" (see chapter 11), aftermath stories and news features may be highly perishable. When writing such a story, a reporter may find little time for editing, thus he must use an abbreviated method: Read over the story thoroughly and look for the obvious flaws:

Is the lead effective? A strong lead may overcome other problems that may result from a hastily written piece. Take the time to shore up the lead, even if this doesn't allow time for any other editing or rewriting.

Is the reader flow smooth and natural throughout? Pencil in stronger transitions, or pencil out a bogged-down sentence or paragraph. Considering the time factor, if you don't have time to carefully improve a weak section, it is often better to simply delete it, unless the paragraph is absolutely vital to the story.

Is the grammar correct throughout? A dangling modifier or a disagreement between a subject and a verb can be fixed with the quick stroke of a pencil.

Is the story effectively organized? You may not have enough time for a major reorganization, but you may have time to snip and paste a couple of glaring structural flaws.

Are there redundancies? If you have made a "point" once, delete subsequent passages that do nothing but restate that information.

Can key phrases be quickly improved by pencil editing?

Catch style errors and misspelled words in this read-through, *unless* time permits the step which is listed below.

Read over the story once again, *mechanically*, to catch spelling, style, and word use errors.

It should be noted that this step is tedious, demanding and boring. It requires maturity and self-discipline. Yet, in the interest of attaining high professionalism, it must be done to *ensure* accuracy for almost all reporters. Only a very few people are blessed with the talent for perfect spelling and style use.

You must "psych" yourself into a state of mind closely akin to that of a human computer to do this correctly:

Instead of reading sentences, read words. Look at each word as a deadly enemy who is determined to sabotage you by being misspelled or misused.

If you have even the most remote doubt about the word's accuracy, dust off your dictionary and ascertain its spelling and use. Never assume that you know how to spell a word. Many people misspell words for a lifetime because they never take time to look them up. After a few misspellings, a word "looks right" to them, so they never catch it.

In a typical feature story, there should be no more than a half dozen possible stylebook use variations. As you use the stylebook more and more, you will memorize most style usages. Yet, if there is any doubt about the proper stylebook use for a term, take time to look it up.

When carefully applied, this two-step quick editing method is fool-proof. The danger lies in "short-cuts" taken by bored journalists.

If you let your attention drift for even a moment during the second step, you may miss a line or several lines. When your paper is returned, you may see two or three costly spelling errors in a tight group of words, and perhaps two or three other errors in another line further down on your paper. If the story is otherwise error-free, then your eyes probably skipped those lines.

Even using this method, only the most conscientious students turn in error-free papers consistently. Yet, there is no excuse for a single error in a story. It is simply a matter of how much work a student is willing to do to attain high standards.

Editing a Shorter Feature Story Without a Deadline.

Most feature stories fall under this heading. Normally, this includes features ranging from two to four "takes" (pages) that are written in a reporter's off-deadline "free" time.

Basically, this technique of editing is an expansion of the quick editing method:

1. Write a rough draft of your story from notes. This rough draft should include all but the most obviously unusable material you have gathered. Although written in story form, the rough draft should serve more as an elaborate outline than as an attempt at pounding out an early version of the final story.

The rough draft should accomplish these tasks:

Consolidate the material you have gathered in an easily-retrievable form.

Help the writer to firm up a broad story idea into an interesting and workable concept. It's an idea-producer.

Serve as a starting point. As was discussed in earlier chapters, "getting started" is often a major obstacle in writing. With a rough draft under his belt, the writer will often find it easy to start the real story.

2. Edit the rough draft to delete all material that isn't directly relevant to the story angle. You will find that you received basically the same information from several sources, so you simply choose the best, most interesting and authoritative version. Other material may have no bearing on the *real* story. Wield the editing pencil ruthlessly because removal of irrelevant material in the rough draft will save time and work later, when you rewrite and re-edit.

3. Look for "holes," inconsistences and inaccuracies in the rough draft. In examining the information you have gathered, ask yourself these questions:

Are any key questions raised, but left unanswered? If so, you must do more research.

Does material from different sources contradict? If so, you must again contact these sources to try to clear up contradictions.

Is the information accurate? Names, addresses, ages, titles, quotations, and explanations must be accurate. If you have any doubt, doublecheck.

Does your instinct tell you that something is missing? Most reporters quickly learn to heed that "inner voice" that tells them that something is missing or something is wrong. Try to identify the source of that uneasy feeling, and try to satisfy your instinct.

The Rewrite or Final Draft.

The number of steps between the draft and the final story form depends entirely on the writer. Some reporters can, routinely, write a final copy from the draft form. Skilled and experienced reporters often skip even the rough draft. They can crank out an excellent feature story on the first try from notes, then lightly edit it. Experience, time, difficulty of the subject matter, and individual skill determine the number of rewrites.

A journalism student should not confuse laziness with well-founded confidence. Most professionals will, time permitting, resort to at least one rewrite for the good reason that any reporter "worth his salt" can improve any story with a rewrite. It's a matter of professional pride. For journalism students, a rewrite is a valuable learning tool because it forces him to carefully examine each phrase for effectiveness and search for better ways of expression.

Here are the steps of rewriting:

An overriding rule is to never break your concentration once you begin. Don't stop to look up spelling and style, you can catch such errors by editing. And don't allow anyone to interrupt your work. Reporters frequently chase away human interruptions with varying degrees of tact.

The logic behind this rule is that, once you start the creative process, a valuable idea or line of thought may be lost forever because of an avoidable distraction. While a reporter learns to tune out the chaotic noise of the newsroom, such as a ringing telephone on his desk, he can still be distracted by a co-worker who simply wants to chat for awhile.

Concentrate on the lead. After typing up the rough draft, the reporter should have a firm idea of what he will try to say. He has the material for the lead, so, once a strong lead is written, the rest should follow naturally.

In editing the rough draft, the reporter may have removed transitions and background for subsequent paragraphs. The draft final story must flow smoothly and logically, so the reporter must smooth over the lumps that resulted from editing.

Editing the Non-Deadline Feature

The editing process is very similar to that used in deadline features. The main difference is the available time:

> Read over the story carefully, making corrections in grammar, story flow, and phrasing. If the story structure is faulty, take time to chop and paste to correct the problem. If a major segment requires rewriting to avoid "bogging down," then take time for this rewrite.
>
> Once again, read the story mechanically, word by word, and view each word as a deadly enemy. As noted before, doublecheck each word that could conceivably be misspelled.
>
> Let the story "sit" overnight before you hand it in. Then, on the next day, read it over one last time.
>
> The last reading will provide a safety catch to eliminate those unfortunate errors that occur when your eyes skip a line.

Editing Long Features

Personal profiles, full page "takeouts," and other longer feature story forms can be extremely difficult to structure and edit. A 20-page story may be accompanied by 40 pages of rough draft notes.

Since such features often require weeks or sometimes months of hard research, no reporter would even consider anything less than top quality writing. Systematic, painstaking rewriting and editing is especially essential in longer features because of obvious problems with organization and the difficulty of sustaining a strong reader-flow without bogging down somewhere in the 20 or so pages.

> A systematic approach to editing such features can be elaborate:
>
> Type up your notes. Don't waste time in a futile attempt to force these notes into rough draft form. You aren't ready yet.
>
> After typing notes, paste all the pages together, end on end. Then read through the notes, bracketing and labeling groups of material. For example, one passage of notes may deal with the physical description of a key character. Further in the notes, another, then another, passage may also describe him.

As a time-saver you may use numerals to key in groups of material. On a separate piece of paper, you may write:

1 — Description of Miller
2 — Death penalty philosophy
3 — Co-worker's evaluation of Miller
4 — Personal history of Miller
5 — Campaign anecdotes
6 — Drug controversy

Since the material will often be repeated in the notes, or it may be elaborated on, the numbers beside brackets enable quick identification.

Outline the story. At this stage, you should have a rough idea of the story you want to write. This tentative outline will guide you through the first draft.

Use scissors or a straight ruler to chop up the typed notes, according to bracketed groupings. Since these groupings have already been keyed by numbers, you have only to stick them into appropriate piles that correspond with the keys.

Examine each stack of groupings carefully, and throw away the obvious redundancies and material that is obviously not relevant to the story. Then, paste together the surviving groups of information according to the outline.

At this point, you have already accomplished some early editing by discarding unusable material well before even the rough draft stage. You have consolidated your notes into manageable proportions and arranged them so that the rough draft will, in effect, write itself.

Write a rough draft, using the re-arranged notes and the working outline. In this draft, concentrate on finding a working lead—not necessarily the final, polished lead—and on gluing together these groupings with smooth writing and good transitions.

Mercilessly edit the rough draft, deleting redundancies that slipped through the initial chop-and-paste stage. Examine each anecdote and informational block for relevance. Ask yourself whether each given block really furthers your goal of telling the story. If the answer is "no," then pencil it out.

The story notes have now been boiled down to the essentials and arranged into a tentative structure. Now, you are ready to tackle the writing chore.

Make a final outline. In writing the draft, you should have developed a better feel for the arrangement needed to effectively tell the story. Read over the draft carefully to spot structural problems, then accommodate corrections on the final outline.

Rewrite final draft. As noted earlier, the number of rewrites—if any—depend on many variables. Regardless of the number of rewrites needed before the story is ready to be handed in, the procedure remains basically the same:

After each rewrite, read over the story carefully to determine flaws in grammar, phrasing and story flow. Eliminate such errors through rewrites or editing.

Be especially aware of structural problems. If major structural weaknesses exist, then the story must again be rewritten.

Final Story Form

After working several days on a long feature story, the last obstacle is the small inaccuracy that can sabotage an otherwise excellent piece. While the word-by-word reading-editing chore is painful for shorter features, it is exhausting, sometimes maddening, in the long feature. Yet, it is even more important in longer features, because more is at stake.

Because of the great length, a reporter may be well advised to perform the word-by-word editing in sections. If fatigue is distracting you, make a small pencil mark to indicate where you stopped, then take a break.

Once again, let the story "sit" overnight, then read it over again to catch the errors that result from mental fatigue.

Summary

While there is nothing glamorous about the nitty-gritty work of editing and polishing a feature story, the necessity of such work cannot be over-emphasized. Keep in mind that a reporter's reputation literally is at stake whenever a story appears under his by-line. While these editing methods may be altered to fit your own needs and style, you must retain some sort of system so that your by-line will be synonymous with top-quality, professional writing.

Applying Polishing Techniques

The gap between theory and practice is a perilous one for many students. To aid in this transition, let's take a feature story at rough notes stage and follow it through the editing and rewrite process.

Rough Notes

As police beat reporter, you have gained the confidence of Detective Clark B. McComb, a narcotics investigator. With the permission of their supervisor, Clark and his partner, Detective Richard Franklin, allow you to join them to observe "the life of a narc" for a feature story.

You have ridden with them before to gain background knowledge and to cover major narcotics raids, so you are familiar with their method of operation. Using "street sources"—underworld contacts that you have made—you also know that both officers are honest and well respected by their drug-pushing adversaries.

At 7:30 p.m., you meet Clark and Richard in the Capitol City Police Organized Crime Control Bureau:

"You picked a good night," Clark said, grinning. "We're going to hit Charlie Evans' place. We have search warrants, so we won't have any problems.

"Charlie has gotten too ambitious. He's selling coke (cocaine) to high school kids, now. Several parents have complained, so we were able to get enough testimony to convince the grand jury."

While Clark telephones an informant to gain more information about another narcotics ring, you jot down observations of the detectives' physical description and information you've gathered.

At 8 p.m., you climb into the back of an unmarked police cruiser and Clark drives out of the police parking lot while Richard radios police units in the vicinity of Evans' house.

"Stay off the 900 block of West Fifth Avenue until you hear from us," Richard told a uniformed police crew. "When we're ready, you can come in to back us up."

During the 10-minute drive to Evans' house, McComb and Franklin joke and tease each other with rollicking humor. They swap anecdotes about past raids, emphasizing goofs by the other detective. In a moment of insight, you perceive that the officers are joking to relieve tension. Franklin admits it, explaining, "This is one of the most dangerous jobs in police work.

"According to the law, we must identify ourselves as police before the dope dealer is obliged to let us in. It's rare that one will simply open the door and say, 'Come on in fellows.'

"Most of the time, we can hear them scrambling to the commode where they try to flush down the evidence (drugs). Then, we hit the door (break it down) and try to beat them to the commode.

"Sometimes, though, we get a different reception. We've both been shot at several times. They shoot right through the door. You can get killed that way."

Each officer tells hair-raising stories about gunplay, with hilarious accounts of the frightened reactions of his partner.

At 8:10 p.m., the car stops a half block from Evans' house and you quietly follow the officers to the front door. You stand behind Mc-Comb as he and Franklin position themselves on either side of the door, carefully standing away from the area directly in front. You notice that Franklin is holding a sledge hammer.

McCombs rings the door bell.

"Who is it?" a voice on the other side asks.

"Police, open up. We have a warrant!" McCombs shouts.

When fleeing footsteps were heard through the door, McComb stepped back, then threw his full weight behind his right foot which struck the door, heel first, inches from the doorknob. He bounced back from the door, and landed in an unceremonious heap.

Franklin laughed so hard that he could barely swing the heavy sledge hammer, which tore through the door, removing the doorknob and lock. A second swing smashed an inside lock at the top of the door.

"This blasted door is two inches thick," McComb grumbled as he dashed inside. Halfway down the hall, McComb heard the roar of a commode. He reached the bathroom just in time to see Evans frantically pressing the flush lever.

Grinning broadly, McComb extracted a large, plastic bag from the commode. The bag was filled with a fine, white, crystalline powder.

"This idiot didn't have enough sense to open the bag," McComb said, triumphantly. "It was too big to flush down."

While the detectives searched the house for other drugs, you sat with the miserable Evans in his living room. Evans thought that you were a new narcotics detective. He confidently told you, "They won't find nothing, you're wasting your time. You got it all." He nervously lit a cigarette, forgetting that another was already burning in the ashtray.

A half hour later, Franklin yelped with joy. He walked down the stairs holding another plastic bag filled with white powder.

"Evans, you're the lowest critter I've ever seen," he said, grinning. "Imagine, hiding $25,000 worth of 'coke' in a baby shoe. Is that any way to raise a kid?"

The door suddenly opened and both Franklin and McComb swiftly drew their revolvers. They lowered the guns when Evans' wife and two children walked in.

"What's going on here?" Mrs. Evans asked angrily.

McComb politely explained that Evans was under arrest for possession of narcotics for sale. He reassured her that she would not be arrested, although she was technically an accomplice.

"Somebody has to look after these kids," McCombs explained.

After taking Evans into custody, the detectives turned him over to a uniformed police crew for transportation to the jail, then headed back to headquarters to turn in evidence and reports.

Suddenly, Franklin yelled, "There goes Flathead Wilson. I think there's an A&B warrant (assault and battery) out for him. McComb turned around to follow Wilson's car as Franklin radioed for a check of records to determine if Wilson was wanted.

"We have an active A&B warrant on William Edward Wilson, 34, of 1608 22 Street," a voice blared over the radio.

Franklin stuck a portable emergency light atop the car as Mc-Comb accelerated, to pursue Wilson's Cadillac. Wilson, apparently unaware of the pursuit, pulled into the parking area of an abandoned hamburger stand. The detectives' car squealed to a halt alongside.

Wilson saw the flashing red light, then "gunned" his engine. The baby-blue Cadillac leaped forward. McComb steered his 6-cylinder car into the Cadillac's path to cut off the escape, but jammed on the brake when it was apparent that the Cadillac would not stop.

Cursing softly, McComb steered his car into a course of pursuit. The Cadillac ran through a stop light, then picked up speed with the police car straining to keep up.

"The city is so blasted cheap that they won't give us a big engine," Franklin explained as he braced himself for a squealing curve.

"Crew 42 to dispatch," Franklin called into the radio. "We're in pursuit of a 1975 Cadillac El Dorado, light blue, license GY—2331, on MacArthur Street heading north toward 23rd. Can you set up a block?"

The radio crackled frantically as the dispatcher positioned cruisers to cut off the escape.

Suddenly, Franklin cursed bitterly. "He just turned each on 21st., can you reposition?"

The red tail lights of the fleeing Cadillac were becoming smaller as the distance between the Cadillac and police widened. Finally, the Cadillac left city limits and turned onto a deserted county road. The dispatcher called for help from the Sheriff's department.

"Flathead has dope in that car, or else he wouldn't run like this," McComb speculated. "There was a second person in the car, too. I think it was a woman."

"If he had any dope, it's gone now," Franklin said, sadly. "He's ditched it out the window."

The tail lights had disappeared, but McComb drove on, hoping that he would see them again on a long, straight stretch ahead. He grumbled disappointedly when no tail lights were in sight. Instead, a lone car came toward the police car, going the other direction. As the bright headlights flashed by, Franklin turned and said, "That's him! He doubled back on us."

McComb turned to follow the familiar tail lights as Franklin radioed to set up a new roadblock. Several miles down the road, the officers saw a roadblock of Sheriff's cars. The Cadillac had pulled to the side of the road a hundred yards from the roadblock.

The scene was chaotic. Wilson had leaped from the car and run into a thicket of trees, leaving his hapless girlfriend behind. Sheriff's deputies were chasing him.

Several other police and Sheriff's cars pulled up as McComb and Franklin talked to the deputy who was left behind to guard the woman.

"He's a real gentleman, leaving this lady behind like that," the deputy said, chuckling. "I've radioed in for an identification check on the lady. She refuses to talk, but I used her driver's license. She's awfully mad about all this."

The deputy walked to his car to receive a radio report, then returned with a broad grin.

"And this ain't no lady, she's an armed robber," he said. "Yeah, there's an armed robbery call out on her."

McComb and Franklin laughed, then peered into the dark trees where Wilson had fled. Another deputy came over with another newsy tidbit.

"The dispatcher just told us a farmer nearby called to say that officers had better stay off his land," the deputy said. "The farmer has been listening to our radio traffic and he's scared. So he said he'd shoot anything that runs near his house. We're warning our officers to stay away."

McComb and Franklin laughed until they were breathless.

"I sure hope old Flathead takes a shortcut across that farm," Franklin said, gasping for breath. "He'll be picking buckshot out of his hide for a month."

You asked the detectives why they weren't joining the chase.

"No use getting our shoes muddy," McComb said, chuckling. "Besides, I'd hate to be shot by a deputy who didn't know I was lurking in the woods."

The officers hopped into their car and drove back toward headquarters.

"You may wonder why we're leaving," Franklin said. "The case is out of our hands, now. The sheriff's deputies now have jurisdiction since we're no longer in hot pursuit. If they catch him, they'll turn him over to us. The woman is their prisoner, too."

"Any way you look at it, Flathead has had a bad day," McComb said, grinning. "He's lost his Cadillac, his woman, and probably a few thousand dollars of dope."

"Yeah," Franklin said. "I can just see him coming out on the other side of the woods with his $75 alligator shoes muddy and soggy, his $300 suit ripped up by thorns, his lungs aching from the run, and his body smelling like he hasn't had a bath in a month."

"Man, will he be cussing us," McComb said, as they both howled.

Returning to the newsroom, you have ample material for an excellent news feature story. Your notes are scrawled and sketchy, since you had to scribble wildly in the dark as the police car swerved unnervingly down the road. You must rely on your memory to fill in details around those basic notes. Earlier interviews with street sources resulted in more complete notes.

Typing up your notes, this material emerges:

INTERVIEW WITH PETE GRAHAM, JUNKIE (no name)

Graham: "Those two dudes (McComb and Franklin) are straight as they come. The word is that a bribe will land you in the slammer (jail). They don't scare, either. Before they hit Luke Simms' operation last year, they had been told that Luke would have them wasted (killed). They went ahead, anyhow.

"For narcs, they're good dudes. They don't bother a junkie unless he's selling stuff (dope). Man, when you're on it, no jail term can get you off it. They know that, so they don't harass."

INTERVIEW:DONNA FARROW, PROSTITUTE-JUNKIE

Donna: "Those guys are super straight, Yeah, they've busted (arrested) me a couple of times, but it wasn't on funky (flimsy) evidence, they had me good.

"Did you know that they buy Christmas presents for kids of junkies they've sent up (sent to prison)? Yeah, they pass the hat to other cops, then go out and buy presents. McComb dresses up as Santa. Lots of kids wouldn't get a thing except for the narcs."

Note: Above information confirmed by Johnny (bookie), Andy Sidwell, Rhonda McMann and Benny O.

NIGHT WITH NARCS' NOTES

Description:
McComb: 26 years old, white, long brown hair with full beard. Dressed in blue sports coat, white turtle-neck, about 6-2, 200 pounds. Brown eyes.

Franklin, 25 years old, black, moderate Afro and Vandyke beard. He's 6-1, 225 pounds. Very muscular. Round face.

Background Note: Despite some racial tension within the police department, the two narcs are inseparable friends.

McComb: "Rich and I just talked it out one night on a stake-out. We don't agree about some things, but we really are good friends. We've agreed that busting the low-down rogues who sell dope to kids—black and white kids—is more important than hassling each other."

Franklin (teasing): "Yeah, and besides, Clark-the-Narc loves soul food, so he's not all bad."

ORGANIZED CRIME CONTROL UNIT OFFICE

Large, open room with 22 desks crowded together to accommodate detectives who work on narcotics, gambling, vice, and criminal intelligence (gathering information on organized crime). Franklin's desk is in perfect order with reports stacked neatly in In-Out baskets. McComb's desk is in frightful disarray, with papers strewn an inch deep. On the wall behind their desk is a sign that lists maximum prison sentences for each narcotics-related offense.

Franklin: "You'd be surprised how cooperative a suspect gets when he sees this sign and starts totalling up the years."

RIDE WITH NARCS

Suspect: Charles Evans, 41, of 923 W. Fifth St. Warrant for search. Arrested and charged with possession of narcotics for sale. Found: 2 bags of suspected cocaine (lab tests pending, but narcs say it's for real) worth about $50,000 at street sale prices, maybe more, depending on quality.

Arrest came at 8:15 p.m. Left headquarters at 8 p.m. On the way, told stories about previous raids, including ones I've witnessed. Some of best:

Last Jan., McComb took front door and Franklin back door in raid. Suspect was giant of a man, violent tendencies. Two uniformed crews (4 policemen in all) joined the raid. Two went with McComb and two with Franklin.

Franklin: "McComb faked me out. He knew that the dude would take the back door, so he gave it to me. (McComb laughs). As soon as Clark said 'Police,' the dude flew out the back door and ran right over Brooks and Sanders (two uniformed officers). They slowed him down just enough, so I lowered my head and tackled him head-on. It knocked the wind out of him long enough for us to get the handcuffs on. But my neck was hurting for a week after that."

Second anecdote. McComb: "Serves you right. Remember the Turner raid? (Franklin laughed). Rich developed some solid information that there was an acid (LSD) lab over on East Third Street in a garage. I was supposed to make a buy, then Rich and uniformed officers would move in for the bust.

"Rich swore that the operators were from out of town, so they wouldn't know me. So, I sashayed into the garage, real cool-like, and asked this guy if I could buy $50 worth of acid. He said he didn't know what I was talking about, so I said, 'Come on man, you know, acid, LSD.'

"Then he picked up a hammer and backed me against the wall and yelled to his wife to call police. Rich's absolutely reliable informant set me up. The man is a preacher! I sure had a lot of explaining to do."

Franklin: (response to question) "Yeah, we get threatened all the time. I can't even list all the people who have said they'd waste us. But as long as they're making threats, I don't worry about them doing anything. If they stop making threats, then I'll worry because then they're serious about it."

(After raid, before chase), Franklin: "Before I was assigned to narcotics, I used to think that Clark and the other narcs got carried away with their jobs. You know, they're obsessed with getting the dealers (major drug suppliers).

"Now that I've worked with Clark for about a year, I feel the same way he does. I know it's an obsession, but you can't help it. After you've seen a few 16-year-old junkies (drug users) and you've seen what that stuff is doing to people, you take it personally. A drug pusher is the absolute worst sort of human filth in the world. God help us if we can't stop drug traffic. I mean that literally, God help us."

McComb: (response to question) "Yeah, my wife and kids worry about me, but they've learned to live with it. I've been shot twice. Each time, Norma pleaded with me to go back to uniform patrol. It's rough on her and the kids because I'm never home. We work 60 hours a week lots of time without being paid for 20 of it. But I keep thinking, what if some pusher sold drugs to my kids? Everytime I see a 14-year-old junkie I think about my kids and it makes me mad."

Franklin: (same question) My wife worries, sure, but I don't have any kids. I do have three cousins who are strung out on heroin. Yeah, I take a very personal interest in my job because they were good kids. My wife understands."

RAID NOTES

8 p.m., left police HQ in unmarked, 6-cyl. green Chevy.
8:01, Franklin advises crews to stay off 900 block W Fifth.

8:10, pull up half block each of Evans' House. Detectives check revolvers, radio backup units to move in in 5 minutes.

Franklin carries sledge hammer to door. "It comes in handy because some of these places are harder to get into than Fort Knox."

8:12, McComb rings doorbell. "Who is it?"—"Police, open up. We have a warrant."—McC. . . . shuffling of footsteps. McC. kicks door, bounces off. McC. rushes in, gun drawn, after Franklin hits door with sledge. Catches Evans in bathroom, flushing. Bag too big. Filled with fine, white, crystalline powder—cocaine.

"This idiot didn't have enough sense to open the bag," McC. "It was too big to flush down."

Search for more drugs. "They won't find nothing, you're wasting your time," Evans. "You got it all." Half hour later (8:45) Franklin yelps, comes downstairs with another bag. "Evans, you're the lowest critter I've ever seen. Imagine hiding $25,000 worth of coke (cocaine) in a baby shoe. Is that any way to raise a kid?"

Door opens, detectives draw revolvers, lower when Evans' wife, two children walk in. Mrs. Wanda Evans, 27, Lillian, 9, Ricky, 7.

"Whats going on?" Mrs. E. McC. explains, no charges against her.

"Somebody has to look after these kids," McC.

9 p.m., Evans taken to jail by uniformed crew.

CHASE

9:15 Franklin sees light blue Cadillac. Driver: William Edward "Flathead" Wilson, 34, of 1608 22 Street. McC. turns around while Franklin checks, confirms A&B warrant. Pursue with flashing red light—no siren. Cadillac pulls into lot of abandoned hamburger stand. McC pulls alongside. Wilson sees police, lurches forward. McC tries to block but stops to avert collision (with civilian reporter in car). Chase begins. Franklin radios to set block at 23rd st. Chase on MacArthur, 75 m.p.h. "The city is so blasted cheap that they won't give us a big engine," Franklin. Cadillac turns before roadblock. Chase on County Road 157 at 130 m.p.h. Sheriff's deputies set up block. Taillights disappear, McC drives on. Headlights. Turn around, Cadillac doubled back and passed.

Ahead can see Cadillac pulled over 100 yards short of block. Door is open. Deputy is talking to woman. Three Sheriff's Dept. cars there. Wilson had split, leaving girlfriend. Deputies chasing him on foot.

Deputy: "He's a real gentleman, leaving this lady behind like that." Walks off, returns with identification check report on woman: "And this ain't no lady, she's an armed robber. Yeah, there's an armed robbery call out on her." (Note: she's wanted as a suspect in the Jan. 14 robbery of Jones' Wine Shop.)

Deputy 2: "The dispatcher just told us a farmer nearby called to say that officers had better stay off his land. The farmer has been listening to radio traffic and he's scared, so he said he'd shoot anything that runs near his house. We're warning our officers to stay away."

Franklin: "I sure hope old Flathead takes a shortcut across that farm. He'll be picking buckshot out of his hide for a month."

Q.—Why aren't you chasing? Answer: Sheriff's jurisdiction now.

"Any way you look at it, Flathead has had a bad day. He's lost his Cadillac, his woman, and probably a few thousand dollars of dope." McC.

Franklin: "Yeah, I can just see him coming out on the other side of the woods with his $75 alligator shoes muddy and soggy, his $300 suit ripped up by thorns, his lungs aching from the run, and his body smelling like he hasn't had a bath in a month."

McC: "Man, will he be cussing us."

In typing out the notes, the reporter made no attempt to fill in details. The adventure is still very fresh in his mind, so the notes act as keys to open these areas of memory. Also, some extraneous material was deleted and some additional material was inserted after the reporter checked with the officers later to fill informational holes. The notes, as written, are a fairly realistic sample of notes taken by a reporter under similar circumstances. However, many words which were spelled out fully in this version, would normally be abbreviated in reporter's notes.

The Rough Draft

Although this story would normally require writing under deadline because of the highly-perishable news elements within it, a reporter for an afternoon newspaper may find sufficient time to allow for at least one rewrite before the noon deadline because the material is available when he arrives at his desk at 7:30 a.m. In this case, he may use the method for editing shorter features without a deadline.

The rough draft, as you will recall, uses almost all of the material gathered and serves as an elaborate outline of the final story to come. In this case, the story basically tells itself.

Here is a rough draft version. Paragraphs are numbered for notes of reference following the draft:

1. Standing to the left side of the front door as a precaution against an unexpected volley of bullets, Detective Clark McCombs rang the doorbell and announced, after someone said "Who is it," "Police, open up. We have a warrant."

2. At the sound of retreating footsteps. McComb kicked the door beside the doornob and bounced back, tumbling into a heap. His

partner, Detective Richard Franklin, laughed so hard he could barely swing the sledge hammer which splintered the door at the doornob. A second swing demolished an inside top lock.

3. McCombs cursed the "two-inch thick" door as he rushed inside, followed by Franklin, with guns drawn. They heard the flushing of a commode—a widely-used method of destroying drug evidence—and McComb ran to the bathroom where he found the suspected drug dealer trying to flush down a plastic bag of fine, white, crystalline powder that McCombs said may be cocaine.

4. McComb plucked the bag out, laughed and said, "This idiot didn't have enough sense to open the bag. It was too big to flush down."

5. The arrest of Charlie Evans, 41, of 923 W. Fifth St. on suspicion of possession of narcotics for sale was routine business in the life of narcotics detectives for Capital City Police's Organized Crime Control Unit.

6. Armed with search warrants obtained after weeks of investigation, Franklin and McCombs have been impeded by locked doors so many times that they carry a sledge hammer along as a back-up to swift, physical kicks.

7. "It comes in handy because some of these places are harder to get into than Fort Knox," Franklin explained as he gripped the sledge hammer.

8. McComb and Franklin, nicknamed "salt and pepper" by fellow officers, are markedly different men in many respects who share a common bond that has welded them together in strong friendship: a hatred of drugs.

9. Franklin, 25, is a burly black man at 6 feet 1, 225 pounds, with a moderate Afro hairstyle and a physique that would make a pro football coach eager to convert him from "narc" to fullback. A pro football scout, however, would take one look at Franklin's ever-present smile and scratch his name off the list because he's not mean enough.

10. The same pro scout may have second thoughts if he could see Franklin's menacing scowl when he talks about "low-down rogues" who sell dope to kids.

11. McComb, 26, is a lanky 6 feet 2, 180 pounds, with long brown hair and a full beard. He looks and talks like a stereotype "acid head" of a decade ago. His dark brown eyes stare with the coldness that comes from seeing and dealing with the worst that humanity has to offer, day after day.

12. But there is no coldness in McComb's eyes when he jokes and teases with Franklin. Despite racial tension within the police department, the two officers seem inseparable, other officers said.

13. "Rich and I just talked it out one night on a stake-out. We don't agree about some things, but we really are good friends.

14. "We've agreed that busting the low-down rogues who see

dope to kids—black and white kids—is more important than hassling each other."

15. Franklin listened, nodded, then grinned and said, "Yeah,
and besides, Clark-the-Narc loves soul food, so he's not all bad."

16. During the Evans raid, the two "narcs" worked together
instinctively, without exchanging words. As Evans nervously fidgeted
and lit one cigarette while another smouldered in an ash tray, the
detectives methodically searched the house for more suspected
drugs.

17. With a yelp of satisfaction, Franklin carried a second,
similar bag downstairs to where Evans was sitting in the living
room and said, "Evans, you're the lowest critter I've ever seen.

18. "Imagine, hiding $25,000 worth of coke (cocaine) in a
baby shoe. Is that any way to raise a kid?"

19. The front door suddenly opened and the detectives
swiftly drew their revolvers and pointed them at the door. When
Evans' wife, and two children, aged 9 and 7, walked in, they
lowered the guns.

20. McCombs gently calmed Mrs. Evans and assured her that
she would not be arrested. "Somebody has to look after these
kids," he explained.

21. At 9 p.m., the detectives turned Evans over to two uniformed officers who were waiting outside, then returned to their
car to drive to headquarters to make out reports.

22. The tension of the raid was over, but the narcs were still
keyed up. Living in day-to-day danger creates tell-tale signs of
nervousness that were apparent in the joking and teasing that
occurred enroute to the raid.

23. During that 10-minute drive, the detectives laughed about
follies that occurred on previous raids. The laughter had the effect
of somehow lessening the danger.

24. Franklin recalled that McCombs had outmaneuvered him
in one raid, in which the suspect was a giant of a man with violent tendencies.

25. "He knew that the dude would take the back door (for
his escape) so he gave it to me.

26. "As soon as Clark said 'Police,' the dude flew out the
back door and ran right over (George) Brooks and (Peter) Sanders (uniformed officers).

27. "They slowed him down just enough, so I lowered my
head and tacked him head-on. It knocked the wind out of him long
enough for us to get the handcuffs on. But my neck was hurting
for a week."

28. Franklin countered soon afterwards by sending McComb
into a suspected garage LSD laboratory where McComb was to buy
the drug for evidence.

29. "I sashayed into the garage, real cool-like, and asked this
guy if I could buy $50 worth of acid (LSD)," McCombs said.

30. Instead, the man threatened him with a hammer and yelled for his wife to call police.

31. "The man is a preacher," McComb explained, giggling. "I sure had a lot of explaining to do."

32. Both officers admitted that the job is dangerous, and that they receive many threats. Franklin dismissed the threats, saying, "If they stop making threats, then I'll worry because then they're serious about it."

33. The dangers sometime catch up with the officers. Mc-Combs said that he has been shot twice. Both officers have been shot at many times.

34. Despite the dangers involved, the narcotics detectives agreed that their job is so vital that it must be performed, danger or no danger.

35. "Before I was assigned to narcotics, I used to think that Clark and the other narcs got carried away with their jobs," Franklin said. "You know, they're obsessed with getting the dealers (major drug sellers).

36. "Now that I've worked with Clark for about a year, I feel the same way he does. I know it's an obsession, but you can't help it.

37. "After you've seen a few 16-year-old junkies (drug users) and you've seen what that stuff is doing to people, you take it personally.

38. "A drug pusher is the absolute worst sort of human filth in the world. God help us if we can't stop drug traffic. I mean that literally, God help us."

(Insert Family Life)

39. While the dangers of the job cause tensions that emerge in jokes and horseplay between the officers, their wives must live with the tension of never knowing whether their husbands will come home safely. Their tension can't be dissipated with masculine bravado.

40. McComb said that each time he was wounded, his wife pleaded with him to return to uniformed patrol duty, but he refuses to heed her.

41. "It's rough on her and the kids because I'm never home," he said. "We work 60 hours a week lots of time without being paid for 20 of it. But I keep thinking, what if some pusher sold drugs to my kids?"

42. "Everytime I see a 14-year-old junkie, I think about my kids and it makes me mad."

43. To Richard Franklin, the threat of drugs to his family is less hypothetical. "I do have three cousins who are strung out on heroin. Yeah, I take a very personal interest in my job because they were good kids.

44. "My wife understands."

45. Danger has many faces for narcotics officers. Sometimes it

is the face of a speedometer with the indicator needle trembling past 90 m.p.h. as the unmarked police car squeals around curves.

46. And such dangers often pop up unexpectedly, such as on the trip back to headquarters after the Evans raid Tuesday night.

47. At 9:15 p.m., Franklin saw a light blue Cadillac that, to anyone but a policeman, was exactly identical to scores of other light blue Cadillacs in Capitol City. Somehow, Franklin noticed it with his peripheral vision as he chatted with McComb.

48. "There goes Flathead Wilson," Franklin declared.

49. Without hesitation, McComb made a U-turn to follow the Cadillac while Franklin called over the radio for a records check to see if Wilson was still wanted on an assault and battery charge. Wilson is also suspected of dealing in drugs.

50. When a voice on the radio confirmed that Wilson was wanted, Franklin placed a portable flashing red light atop the car while McComb speeded up.

51. The Cadillac pulled into the lot of an abandoned hamburger stand at the corner of Fifth Avenue and MacArthur Street. The driver was apparently unaware of the pursuing police car.

52. McComb pulled in alongside the Cadillac, but, when the driver saw the policemen, he pressed the accelerator ·and the car lurched forward.

53. McComb floored his accelerator in an attempt to block the escape, but he had to slam on his brakes to avoid a collision when it became apparent that the Cadillac driver didn't intend to stop.

54. As the Cadillac squealed onto MacArthur Street, the police fell in behind to take up pursuit. The speedometer needle quickly jumped past 75 m.p.h. as Franklin called over the radio for a roadblock at 23rd Street on MacArthur.

55. But, two blocks before reaching the roadblock, the Cadillac turned left onto 21st Street.

56. McComb muttered angrily as he mashed the accelerator harder in a vain effort to squeeze more speed from the 6-cylinder engine.

57. "The city is so blasted cheap that they won't give us a big engine," Franklin complained.

58. The chase suddenly left the city as the Cadillac roared out County Road 157 at an estimated 130 m.p.h. on straight stretches.

59. As sheriff's deputies joined the chase and set up roadblocks, McComb cursed while the tail lights grew smaller and smaller until, after a slow curve, they had disappeared.

60. McComb drove on, anxiously, hoping to see the elusive red lights on a long straight stretch of road. Moments later, bright headlights whisked toward them, then blurred past.

61. "That's him, he's doubled back on us," Franklin said as he turned to see the familiar tail lights.

62. As McComb made a U-turn, Franklin used the radio to warn deputies of the sudden reversal. A few minutes later, they saw a roadblock ahead and the Cadillac was stopped 100 yards from it.

63. Three sheriff's deputy's cars straddled the road. One deputy guarded the Cadillac and the woman inside while his colleagues scrambled into the forest after Wilson.

64. "He's a real gentleman, leaving this lady behind like that," the deputy said. The crackle of the car radio drew the deputy to his patrol car. After a quick conversation, he returned, grinning.

65. "And this ain't no lady, she's an armed robber," he said, explaining that an identification check had turned up an armed robbery warrant for her arrest as a suspect in the Jan. 14 robbery of Jones' Wine Shop.

66. Other police and deputy's cars arrived and the officers milled around, chatting and waiting.

67. McComb explained that city police couldn't join pursuit because the sheriff assumed jurisdiction in that county area.

68. Another deputy approached and said, "The dispatcher just told us a farmer nearby called to say that officers had better stay off his land.

69. "The farmer has been listening to radio traffic and he's scared, so he said he'd shoot anything that runs near his house. We're warning our officers to stay away."

70. Franklin and McComb looked at each other, grinned, then broke into laughter.

71. "I sure hope old Flathead takes a shortcut across that farm," Franklin said. "He'll be picking buckshot out of his hide for a month."

72. The tension dissipated with the laughter. The danger of a sudden blast of shotgun pellets ripping through a door was past.

73. And McComb was in no mood to steer the car around sharp curves at near-suicidal speeds as he drove back toward police headquarters.

74. Both men plunged into the age-old police method for calming taunt nerves after a brush with deadly danger: rough, boisterous humor.

75. "Any way you look at it, Flathead has had a bad day. He's lost his Cadillac, his woman, and probably a few thousand dollars of dope," McComb said, chuckling.

76. "Yeah," Franklin said, chortling. "I can just see him coming out on the other side of the woods with his $75 alligator shoes muddy and soggy, his $300 suit ripped up by thorns, his lungs aching from the run, and his body smelling like he hasn't had a bath in a month."

77. "Man, will he be cussing us," McComb said with a note of relish.

78. After all, being cussed by a narcotics dealer is a compliment in the strange and deadly world of narcotics detectives.

Analysis

For the most part, the story was written in chronological sequence as an adventure. The story line was so strong and so natural that the writer decided to let it "tell itself" rather than tamper with structure.

However, it should be noted that this is only a draft, not a finished, polished story. Let's examine some weak paragraphs and some writing techniques that lend themselves to elaboration (The numbers are keyed to the paragraphs in the rough draft version):

1. The idea for the lead is to immediately show the tension and the danger of narcotics police work. Yet, this lead fails because it is too wordy and jumpy. The first several words fail to grab the readers' attention. The quotes are used awkwardly. The writer should try another lead.

2. This vital transitional "link" is, again, wordy. It bogs down with Franklin's laughter and the details of the swinging sledge hammer. It is also too long.

3. Again, too long. The details hinder the flow of action.

7. The difficulties of smashing the door should follow this paragraph for natural placement.

9, 10. The comparison to a football player is fine, but the writer over-elaborated. Make the comparison briefly, then leave it alone. The last sentence of paragraph 9 and all of paragraph 10 should be deleted.

13. Break quote after "stake-out" to insert attribution. Attribution should be made in the first paragraph of a multi-paragraph quotation. Note that in such multi-paragraph quotations, repeated attribution is unnecessary if the quotation mark is omitted from the end of each paragraph and inserted at the beginning of the next.

22. Make it "tell-tale", not "tale-tell."

38. As a transition to material relating to the officers' families, the writer calls both wives at this point to insert the following material gleaned from telephone conversations.

(Insert Paragraph 39)

Norma McComb and Faye Franklin agree with their husbands' assessment of the importance of narcotics investigations. But both women said they wished that someone else's husband had the dangerous job.

"The kids miss him, but they don't worry because they don't really understand the danger," Mrs. McComb said.

"I worry a lot," she added. "Whenever I hear that an

officer has been shot while I listen to the radio, it scares me to death. Twice, it was Clark.

"Each day he stays on narcotics, I know that the odds increase that he'll be shot again. Maybè next time he won't survive."

Mrs. Franklin agreed. "Rich never tells me anything, but I know," she said. "When he comes home late and can't go to sleep, I know what that job is doing to him. Yeah, I worry a lot."

(Pick up story at paragraph 40)

48. To avoid possible libel and pre-trial publicity, the writer should avoid using the suspect's name. Several techniques can achieve this effect. You may use only the nickname to soften the identification, insert a fictitious nickname with a note to that effect to the reader, or simply use the first name alone.

68, 69. The direct quotation is somewhat wordy. These paragraphs could be improved by a tight paraphrase.

74. This unattributed explanation is the reporter's observation. As a veteran police reporter, he based this observation on countless conversations with officers. He had used this observation in past stories, quoting policemen to verify this observation. Therefore, in the writer's judgment, this observation is established as fact.

78. The ending is somewhat forced and stilted. The writer tried to avoid ending on a luke-warm quotation in paragraph 77, but only succeeded in adding a couple of questionable lines to the story. A new ending should be contrived.

SUMMARY

The analysis dealt with major points, not with minor problems of phrasing. To improve the story for the final, polished draft, the writer should shorten it by at least a half-page by tightening loose phrasing and deleting weak material.

As you can see through this somewhat tedious process, good journalistic writing rarely flows, effortlessly, from even the most gifted reporter's typewriter. Instead, it requires concentration and dedicated effort to skillfully mold rough surfaces into a fine, readable story.

SUGGESTED EXERCISES

Using the rough draft and notes of criticism, write this story in final polished form.

8   Types of Feature Stories

If you will recall the definition of a feature story as given in Chapter 1, a key element of that definition is that a feature story may or may not have news value.

In the following chapters, we will discuss different types of feature stories, some of what have news value, and some of which do not. Because of this, these types of feature stories will be categorized as either *News Features* or *Human Interest Features*.

A *News Feature* is a perishable story related to a current event or situation that is of interest to the public. It may or may not be the initial story that brings the event to the attention of the public. The news feature seeks to put the event or situation into human perspective and help readers to identify, in human terms, with the story.

A *Human Interest Feature* doesn't have a shred of news value. It is normally not perishable, and it contains no information of vital public interest. Instead, the human interest feature dwells on an appeal to the readers' curiosity about other human beings or about such common areas of interest as pets, unusual things and places, or historical ironies.

Let's examine some of the stories discussed in past chapters to apply this classification.

1. *The narcotics detectives story.* Because of the results of the actions, a high speed chase and a major narcotics arrest, this becomes a news feature. The writer must battle a deadline because events in the story are of immediate public significance.

Without the two news items, the story would have been a human interest feature, since it would have dealt exclusively with satisfying human curiosity about the nature of the strange men and the strange job of narcotics police work.

2. *The night-time street sweeper.* This is a human interest story because it deals exclusively with the strange character of the elderly woman who sweeps sidewalks at 2 a.m.

The woman broke no law, her actions affected only a handful of people, she was not victimized, and, in short, she did nothing to justify news coverage. Yet her fascinating story is certainly deserving of inclusion in the newspapers.

Sometimes a fine line separates news from human interest features, however. The day after she aided in the apprehension of the burglar, the same reporter would have written a news feature, emphasizing her role in preventing a burglary *last night.* Since the news angle is highly perishable —a three-week old, attempted burglary is no longer news—the incident received only passing mention.

3. *The draw-bridge operator.* The *lack* of news was a strong point in the appeal of this story about a man who received no attention for 40 years. Unless the bridge had collapsed, taking the operator with it, no news "peg"—connection to a news story—exists, so this is a human interest story.

4. *The great turkey hunt.* Without the imagination of the reporter, the situation hardly existed. This is a human interest feature.

5. *The plight of the museum of natural history.* This is a news feature because it emphasized a heretofore unknown item of public significance: the museum was in danger of closing for lack of funds. The emphasis of children and animals is a classic human interest feature technique, and, without the financial problem emphasis, it would have been a good human interest story on its own merits.

Now, let's carefully examine human interest and news features:

NEWS FEATURES

The means of conception of the story idea often determines whether the story will be a news feature or a human interest story.

The news feature normally is a spin-off from a news story that the reporter is covering.

A typical example of the creation of a news feature may start with a cryptic police radio call for cruisers to respond to a possible drowning.

A car had plunged into the river with two women inside. Hearing the call over the newspaper's police radio monitor, the city editor quickly dispatches two reporters to the scene.

At the scene, both reporters are immediately concerned with meeting deadlines for the hard news story. Here's what happened:

The car had swerved suddenly over a curb, down a gradual, 50-foot embankment, and into about eight feet of water. Workmen from a nearby plant, who saw the tragedy, rushed to the river to try to help the women.

One woman had climbed safely atop the car, while the other swam downstream away from it. The workmen rescued the woman from atop the car, but were unable to reach the other.

A young policeman arrived moments later and dove into the icy water to try to save the second woman. He had to turn back to save his own life when the strong current threatened to pull him under.

Witnesses were puzzled because the woman made no attempt to swim to shore before she finally went under. Later, police found that the swimmer, daughter of the woman who was rescued, had been under psychiatric care following a serious automobile accident a year ago. She had been very depressed. Her mother told officers that, without a word of warning, her daughter had turned the steering wheel to cause the accident.

The two newspaper reporters swiftly pried information from policemen, witnesses and coroner's investigators. After a quick huddle, one reporter stayed at the scene as firemen attempted to recover the body, while the second drove to the hospital to try to talk to the survivor and the family. The reporter who stayed at the scene took over news coverage, while his colleague pursued a feature story on the human tragedy.

The reporter who sought the feature story, an accomplished master of human interest features, used the family minister as an informational conduit. Through the minister, he was able to contact the family member who was the most composed, thus compassionately leaving the grief-stricken mother alone. He even managed to acquire a picture of the unfortunate daughter.

As a result of the two reporters' efforts, the newspaper carried a page one, lead story that gave the hard news account of the disaster, and, next to the hard news account, ran a sensitive "sidebar" feature story (Chapter 11) about the young woman and the events that apparently drove her to suicide.

When disasters strike, veteran reporters often instinctively look for such news features that translate the cold, impersonal hard news account into human terms.

After a tornado rips through a town, killing scores of people and leaving hundreds homeless, a newsman soon finds that the cold facts cannot, in themselves, tell the story:

> A tornado ripped a half-mile-wide path of death and distruction through Capitol City Tuesday, killing 47 people, injuring 180, and leaving thousands homeless.

In this hard news version, human suffering and death has been coldly relegated to a statistical rendition. The sheer impact of the disaster cannot be captured in a straight news story.

The reporter who has witnessed the aftermath of such a disaster quickly looks for an accompanying feature story to translate the impact into human terms which will allow readers to comprehend and identify with human suffering.

> Clutching a ragged Teddy Bear, 5-year-old Johnny Stevens whimpered and rubbed his eyes in disbelief as he stood next to his mother in the rubble that, only moments ago, was the center of his world—his home.

Few readers could miss the terrible significance of the wind storm as they view it through the horror-filled eyes of a child. Using a news feature approach, the reporter fulfills the job that any journalist must seek to accomplish: he has fully informed his readers by illuminating the truth so that they can comprehend it.

No reporter is immune to human emotions. In researching and writing such a story, even the most cool-headed veteran may struggle to hold back a flood of emotion, at least until his job is done.

To write high quality news features under such chaotic circumstances requires the high professionalism of a dedicated, experienced newsman.

In such reporting, newsmen are often maligned as being insensitive, or accused of exploiting human tragedy for professional gain. Yet "insensitive" reporters and "cold-hearted" policemen have been seen with tears of compassion running down their cheeks.

Not every news feature involves unpleasant subjects. In political coverage during an election campaign, the city hall reporter may write dozens of news features designed to help readers become acquainted with the candidates.

He may write a featurized account of interaction between the candidates and the public during a neighborhood political forum. The issues and the individual candidates' positions may be "old hat," but the colorful and sometimes revealing interplay between them could help voters discern qualities and flaws among the women and men who are seeking positions of public trust.

Other news features may be humorous. A short, featurized account of the arrest of bungling burglars contains a news element because a burglary is a major crime. But the comedy of errors leading to the burglar's arrest provide the opportunity to render the facts in feature writing style, emphasizing the human follies and not the crime.

Still another type of news feature occurs in coverage of a major festive event, such as a fair or a sports spectacular. In such events, a reporter is often assigned to provide "color stories" to supplement news or sports coverage.

The example of the young girl at her first state fair is basically a color story. This form of news feature may or may not contain an element of news, but it is wholly dependent on an event of public interest and it must be written under some deadline pressure before public interest in the event wanes.

Instead of concentrating on the event, itself, the reporter seeks to capture the mood and the peculiar behavior of that strange creature called a crowd.

HUMAN INTEREST FEATURES

The human interest feature is, perhaps, the most common variety of feature story. A reporter's ability to find such a story is dependent only on his imagination and initiative—not on events or circumstances beyond his control.

While only a few newspapers hire reporters solely for feature writing duties, many reporters specialize in this story art-form while performing general assignment reporting.

Most good human interest feature writers are incurable people-lovers. They relish the strange, inconsistent antics of the human race and, to a large degree, earn their livelihoods by astutely observing and reporting these antics.

A human interest story writer often gravitates toward groups of unusual people, of all social levels.

Some human interest story writers have close contacts with the "street" characters: bookies, bartenders, prostitutes, pimps, muggers, petty thieves, drunkards and dope users. While such associations may make the reporter a bit suspect, a writer named Damon Runyon gained considerable fame through his sensitive, often hilarious accounts of such characters:

With one swat of his ham-sized fist, Louie-the-Bear almost decapitated the knife-wielding thug who had the nerve to carry his mugging trade into the safe confines of the Diamond Bar.

Louie—no one knows his real name—has kept such iron-fisted order in the bar at the corner of Eastman Avenue and Mc-Millian Street for the past 15 years that it has become a neutral haven in the roughest neighborhood in town.

The young mugger was obviously a novice at his trade. As he stalked a drunken businessman in a back booth, Louie watched him from the corner of his eye.

When the unsuspecting robber reached for the victim's wallet, Louie vaulted across the bar and charged like a grizzly bear protecting a cub.

The mugger pulled a knife and Louie swung. Plaster fell from the wall as the mugger's unconscious body flew against it with a bone-cracking thud.

Louie didn't bother to call police. He simply picked up the carcass and pitched it into the alley.

The Runyonesque reporter used the incident as a springboard to a fine feature story on a character that most readers would never meet. Such attempted muggings are so common that they aren't newsworthy in themselves. Yet, what self-respecting writer could let a character such as Louie go unheralded?

What strange adventures has Louie experienced, over the years, in his bar-domain? How does he view his customers? How do they see Louie? What kind of man lies beneath that awesome exterior?

A reporter doesn't have to risk bodily harm by venturing into rough neighborhoods in search of human interest stories. Here are some general categories:

Children

Stories about children, especially children in trouble, are high-readership items. Some typical examples of good topics concerning children are:

Children invent a new game called "pickle" which is a cross between baseball and tag.

An 11-year-old orphan is finally adopted.

Children tell a reporter all about their favorite television shows and why they like them.

That very special viewpoint of children is refreshing and entertaining. Television personality Art Linkletter wrote a collection of experiences called *Kids Say the Darndest Things*. Reporters soon learn that this title is very true.

Everyday Disasters

If the readers have, or easily could, experience a situation, then the psychological identification with the subject is very strong.

A car stalls in the middle of the busiest intersection in town at rush hour. What motorist hasn't had such nightmares?

A dozen people are trapped in an elevator for an hour. A feature story on the helpless feeling of the trapped riders could appeal to anyone who has ever been in an elevator. It could happen to anyone.

A small boy's head is stuck between banisters until firemen rescue him. Any mother can envision her own child in such a predicament.

Humor

A tuba player falls down during the halftime show of a nationally televised football game.

A thief picks a policeman's billfold after being arrested.

The flag in front of the post office is accidentally flown upside down.

Animals

Like children, animals seem to find a special sympathy among readers.

A lost dog walks 40 miles to return home.

Refugees from Cuba sneak puppy with them.

A pet boa constrictor is lost.

Adventure

A mountain climber tells about being lost in a blizzard near the summit of a mountain.

A local businessman returns from a trip to China.

"Sob Stories"

This is among the most maligned of all newspaper specialties, yet it is one of the surest highreadership items.

In the days of sensationalism, the sob story was a major weapon. The stories are characterized by tales of individual woe and hardluck which should bring tears from anyone's eyes.

It should be emphasized that the reporter is expected to ascertain the accuracy of the woeful tales and, whenever possible, to go an extra step and try to locate a source of aid for the unfortunate.

Some typical "sob story" topics would be:

A young woman commits suicide after nine previous attempts.

An elderly man, once a millionaire, is now penniless.

A family has no Christmas presents for the children.

A family has been evicted with no place to go.

Oddity

If a man bites a dog, it isn't news, it's a human interest story. Inconsistencies, ironies and strange happenings make good human interest features.

Some examples:

An Alcohol, Tobacco and Firearms agent ("revenooer") makes wine as a hobby.

An auto mechanic is a zany inventor.

A man covers his lawn with concrete and paints it green.

In writing a human interest feature story, a reporter should follow these rules to avoid sometimes disastrous pitfalls:

Exercise restraint. Armed with an exciting topic, the writer must sometimes fight the tendency to overstate the story. A family that receives federal Welfare assistance is probably not facing starvation. A slight nosebleed doesn't qualify as "bleeding profusely." A thief who picks a policeman's wallet can hardly be called "clever." Don't lose perspective.

Overwriting is a related problem. After being presented with a story that provides an opportunity for strong writing, the reporter can become so enthralled by his prose that he misses the point of his effort: to clearly communicate a story.

Be accurate. A reporter can severely damage his credibility by stretching his facts or by fabricating material. On multi-source stories, such as a color story in which a reporter interviews dozens of people, he may be greatly tempted to throw in his own amusing observations by creating a fictitious person in the crowd.

The chances of being caught in such fabrications are almost nil. Yet the reporter who lowers his ethics will probably, in the hundreds of stories he will write in the future, bend his ethics once too often.

SUMMARY

The distinction between news features and human interest features is somewhat arbitrary. Some stories are of the boarderline variety. They could be classified as either.

Yet, in coming chapters, you will see this pattern emerge: Human interest features are generally studies in human nature that evolve from observations and initiative by reporters. News features normally require the solid reporting skills of a journalist who has coped with every imaginable type of story under intense deadline pressure. The method of research, much more than the writing, is the dividing point.

EXERCISES

Clip five feature stories from your local newspaper.

1. Categorize them by news or human interest features, and explain why you placed each feature into that category.

2. Analyze them to determine whether, with minor changes, each feature could fit into the other category.

9 Brights

As the name implies, a "bright" is a sunny little story that brightens an otherwise gloomy page filled with an assortment of mayhem, disaster and crisis. It serves as a lump of suger to make more serious information a little more palatable to the depressed reader.

By definition, a bright is a short, terse feature that normally contains a humorous and unusual quirk.

Several examples of brights are to be found in previous chapters. The "worst day in the career of the police officer" is a bright.

News editors, who must try to balance the content of each page, eagerly snatch up brights for use in balancing the page or for use as valuable layout fillers.

Let's slip on the news editor's shoes for a moment. You have a strong front page, except for a three-inch gap created by makeup. You have several options for filling the gap. You can chop a second-rate wire service story and use a news filler. You can toy with makeup to place three inches more of a page-one story. You can insert a public service "box" such as a note alerting readers that city offices will be closed for a holiday.

Or you can use a bright.

Perhaps the police beat reporter stumbled across this gem:

During the previous night, two burglars entered the Capitol City Steel Company, at 33 S. Alworth Drive. They carried a safe from the office and started to load it on a truck. The safe slipped and fell on one burglar's hand, severing a finger tip. The burglars, meanwhile, had tripped a silent burglar alarm and they saw police cruisers approaching. They quickly drove away in a red, 1973 Ford pickup truck, leaving the safe behind.

Fortunately for the burglars, the approaching officers didn't see the get-away. Unfortunately, the burglars speeded away. Once inside, the investigating officers found evidence of illegal entry through a pried doorlock, and they later found the safe with the fingertip beneath it. They contacted the dispatcher who advised all other officers of the burglary attempt and the missing finger.

Still speeding, the burglars were driving down E. 30th Avenue on the other side of town when a police car pulled them over for exceeding the speed limit. The sharp-eyed officer noticed the bleeding hand of one burglar and then saw that a fingertip was missing. He arrested them.

Arrested were Joseph L. James, 26, of 801 E. 30th Ave., and Adam P. Barker, 28, of 941 E. 32nd Ave. Barker had the injured hand.

While perhaps a little gruesome, such bungling deserves humorous treatment. The reporter delighted the news editor by writing the story as a bright:

> A perfect fingerprint was left behind by burglars who tried to steal a safe from Capital City Steel Co. Sunday night.
>
> The fingerprint was attached to a fingertip left under the heavy steel safe.
>
> The burglars pried a doorlock at about 10 p.m., carried the safe from the office, and dropped it while trying to load it on a truck, police theorize.
>
> Seeing approaching police cars that were alerted by a silent alarm, the burglars drove away, leaving the safe and a fingertip beneath it. Investigating officers found the evidence, police said.
>
> At 10:30 p.m., Ptl. Joe Williams stopped a speeding red pick-up truck on E. 30th Avenue and arrested Joseph L. James, 26, of 801 E. 30th Ave. and Adam P. Barker, 28, of 941 E. 32nd Ave.
>
> Both men were charged with burglary. Barker was treated for hand injuries, including a missing index fingertip, at Mercy Hospital.

FINDING A BRIGHT

In most cases, brights are found on busy news beats, sometimes hidden in the bulk of hard news items.

The police blotter is a favorite source of brights. The blunders of criminals and the oddities of crimes are often easily written in bright style.

In the example above, the reporter could easily overlook a routine "blotter" offense report about an attempted burglary. Yet, if he listens to police gossip, the unusual aspects of the case will quickly make rounds within the police station.

"Hey, we *really* have Adam Barker now," an officer may say.

"The burglar? How did you get him?" a colleague may ask.

The chuckling story-teller would then relate the events with appropriate laughter at the burglar's expense. Few alert reporters could miss the item.

Public meetings are also good sources, particularly when there is light by-play between public figures. City Hall reporters can land such gems as this:

Tactfulness is next to cleanliness in the code of City Commission politics.

While protest groups are common fare at commission meetings, one such delegation caused a visible outbreak of tongue-biting among city fathers.

"Sometimes, it's better to bite a tongue than to place it in one's cheek," Commissioner Al Moore said later.

"Im an incurable punster," Mayor Charles White later admitted. "I was afraid to open my mouth."

Commissioner Ralph Simon lost his hold on his tongue and, as a result, may have lost votes from the group when he said, "Who's the HEAD of your MOVEMENT?"

The audience laughed at this double-pun. Fellow commission members howled breathlessly. The protest group blushed, en masse, with rage.

The protest group came to present a petition to outlaw pay toilets in public restrooms.

Judicial proceedings may also produce brights.

Judge Foster Allen's dignified countenance remained stoically in place as he meted out strange punishment to the nervous young man who stood before him.

Carl L. Burns, 21, of 1904 N. 20th St. had pleaded guilty to petit larceny Monday in Municipal Court after being charged with the theft of a set of tires from Jones Salvage Yard.

After announcing a six-month sentence in the county workhouse, the judge promptly suspended the sentence "on the condition that you lead an honest and productive life, hereafter.

"Today, you are assuming a great responsibility and a great joy. I wish you and your fiancée every happiness."

Burns quickly embraced Susan Lowe, then led her to the judge's chambers where the wedding ceremony was performed.

WRITING BRIGHTS

In these examples, you will note that information is somewhat sketchy and condensed. No attempt is made to develop personalities or to divulge possibly interesting detail.

The writer knows that success depends on terseness and brevity, so he may even bend writing rules to provide conciseness. In the judicial example, the judge has a "dignified countenance." In other forms of feature stories, the writer would have abided by the rule: show it, don't say it. He would have carefully given physical descriptions that would have conjured a "dignified countenance" in the minds of the readers.

The reason for this exception to the rule lies in the basic objective of any writing: to communicate effectively. In order to communicate the *real* story, it is sometimes necessary to remove the frills and get to the point.

Some brights may include more details, as the story requires, as in the following:

Paul Millian took a Greyhound bus—just as the television commercial suggests—and spent a night in city jail for his trouble.

He neglected to "Leave the driving to us."

Millian, 21, of Oakbark, stopped in the city yesterday to change buses. The Vietnam veteran was returning home.

During the two-hour layover, Millian visited several bars and missed his bus. At 9:50 p.m., Ptl. Joe V. Arns and Ptl. Paul Moore were summoned to the Owl Lounge.

Arns said that Millian was standing on top of the bar, tap-dancing, when the officers entered. They took him into custody.

Noticing service ribbons, including the Purple Heart, that Millian was wearing, Arns and Moore slowly pieced together the story of the soldier's homecoming.

"We felt that after what he had been through, he deserved a break, so we took him to the bus station and told the ticket seller to get him on the next bus to Oakbark," Moore said.

The officers left with a flurry of thank-yous, waves and smiles.

At 10:50 p.m., Moore and Arns heard the police dispatcher notify all units to be on the alert for a stolen Greyhound bus.

"We thought, 'Oh no, he wouldn't,' " Arns said. "But he did."

The bus driver had started the diesel engine to warm it up. As the engine idled, the driver returned to the station to fill out paperwork.

"Millian simply walked to the bus, got inside, and drove off,"

Arns said. "He was drunk, homesick and impatient, so he started home."

The bus was finally stopped by Deputy Carl Voltz on Highway 40, five miles north of the city.

"When I pulled him over, he wouldn't let me in the bus until I paid for the fare," Voltz said. "I had to slip $5 through the driver's window to get on board.

"I got my $5 back after the arrest, though."

Greyhound refused to prosecute the soldier because of the unusual circumstances and because of his service record. Millian was released at 10 a.m. today.

Let's break down the elements of a bright:

The Lead

Before you begin writing a bright lead, remember the peculiarities of the story you are undertaking.

A bright is a very short feature article, so the lead should also be exceptionally short to avoid top-heaviness. A four-line lead on a 25-line story is disproportionately long in appearance, and, since a bright is a short, snappy story, a long lead doesn't properly set the stage for what is to follow.

Secondly, a bright generally has a humorous or unusual quirk— not material of major public interest. Therefore, the writer must quickly grasp the reader's attention, normally through exploiting human curiosity.

With these criteria in mind, an examination of the arsenal of leads available will quickly reveal that one type is made to order for brights: a teaser lead. The teaser lead is the shortest lead form, and it is specifically designed to appeal to human curiosity. The teaser lead simply dangles as fascinating tidbit of information under the reader's nose and forces him to read further to find out what the story is about.

This is much in keeping with still another bright trait: the story lacks details or development. Such popular leads as the descriptive lead, the narrative and, to some degree, the summary require considerable detail.

Other leads may be applicable, depending on the available material. A short, quotation lead can appeal to curiosity, as can a catchy question lead, or a concise direct address lead. Conceivably, a freak lead could set up a bright, but the freak lead normally requires time and space to develop its rather startling and fuzzy theme.

As for combination leads, the time and space needed to combine two feature elements may frequently preclude their use, with the exception of some quotation combinations.

Still another vital ingredient is often found in a good, bright lead: terseness. Brevity in length doesn't necessarily translate into terseness.

A bright lead should move along quickly, in almost a skeleton-like fashion without unnecessary flesh.

In summary, the bright lead must move quickly from the first word, plunging the reader toward the body of the story after nabbing the reader's curiosity. While some other leads may occasionally fit these criteria, the teaser lead is chosen most frequently.

The Body

As any other story, a bright must relate information of interest to the reader. But, while other feature stories have no limit of length, a bright must be written as briefly as possible. While most features allow almost leisurely development of a story theme, the bright is compressed.

A bright may take one of two structural forms: the inverted pyramid or the chronological (suspense) pyramid. As you can see in the illustrations below, however, these pyramids are somewhat different from those illustrated in Chapter 4. The bright pyramids are so compressed that they are "fat."

BRIGHT PYRAMIDS

THE INVERTED PYRAMID.

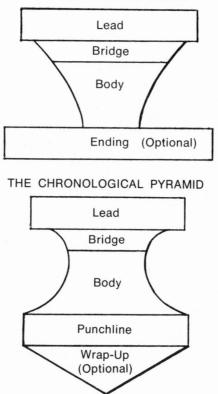

The Inverted Bright Pyramid

After a short, fast-moving lead, the writer quickly moves through the story in descending order of interest and importance, with possibly one exception: the writer may save a key piece to the puzzle created by the lead until the last paragraph.

Using the inverted pyramid to set up an unexpected ending, the writer hopes to surprise the reader. The format may lull the reader by concealing the fact that the story is building to the ending. It heightens the effect of the surprise ending.

The "fatness" of the body is due to the compression of material. Because of the short length and the need to select only vital, interesting information for inclusion in the story, the writer is assuming that the strain of interest to the reader will hold him through the few paragraphs necessary to set up the ending.

A variation is to write the bright without an ending in almost news story fashion. This is normally a poor alternative, because the writer sacrifices the element of surprise. In this variation, the summary lead may be used to quickly wrap-up the basic information relating to a very short, cute item of interest that lacks material for development toward an ending.

Here are examples of inverted bright pyramid variations:

Inverted Bright Pyramid, With Ending

Phillip Morrison MacFlute seemed like any other freshman at Milliard University.

Registered as a journalism major, MacFlute managed to attain a modest C-plus grade average in his coursework, pledged membership in the Kappa Kappa Omega fraternity, and earned an occasional by-line as a campus newspaper reporter.

His professors described him as "the quiet type" who plodded through the courses with just enough effort to win a respectable grade.

While several teachers offered detailed physical descriptions of MacFlute, no two descriptions matched.

MacFlute, you see, has many faces, but none of his own.

MacFlute is a ficticious student created and portrayed by the brothers of the Kappa Kappa Omega fraternity.

"Any institutional system can be beaten, if you know the ropes," Ed Wilks, KKO president said. "Brother MacFlute just beat the system."

End of the story? Not quite.

"MacFlute is engaged to a ficticious sorority girl," Wilks said, grinning, "She will be back next year, after the wedding."

Inverted Bright Pyramid, Without an Ending

Using the same story information, the pyramid may be altered to exclude the ending. The advantage is that this variation is even more compact.

> A ficticious freshman and his phony fiancée have finished a year of college at Milliard University.
>
> Phillip Morrison MacFlute, a creation of the Kappa Kappa Omega fraternity, achieved a C-plus grade average, reported for the campus newspaper as a journalism student, and pledged to the KKO chapter, according to Ed Wilks, fraternity president.
>
> His ficticious fiancée, invented by a sorority, will return for her sophomore year—after their wedding, Wilks said.
>
> MacFlute and his fiancée were portrayed, in classes, by fraternity and sorority members.

The second version, without an ending, was about half as long as the initial version which included an ending. The initial story sacrificed some compactness in the interest of more effective story-telling.

The Chronological Bright Pyramid

In using this format, the writer sets up and delivers the ending like a Bob Hope punchline. An intelligent reader will quickly realize that a "punchline" is coming and, once committed to reading the story, hopefully the reader will anxiously await it.

In the diagram, you will note that the story may continue past the "punchline" if the writer wants to wrap-up loose ends.

A single story can be used as an example of a Chronological Pyramid Bright, with and without wrap-up past the punchline.

> Mrs. Andrew Lewis blushed a little when the greeting card arrived, but U.S. Postal Service officials are mortified.
>
> The greeting card arrived Thursday at the Andrews' 31 Conrad Drive home.
>
> Linda Andrews, 5, walked out to the mailbox picked up the card, and brought it to her mother.
>
> Mrs. Andrews opened the envelope, looked into the curious eyes of her daughter, then blushed when she saw the contents:
>
> The cover of the card showed a bride and a groom beneath large silver bells and gold lettering that read: "Congratulations!"
>
> Then she looked at the postmark and called the Capitol City postmaster.
>
> The card from Ralph Evans, of 2334 Central Ave., was mailed two weeks before the wedding. It arrived just in time for a "big event," but not the right "big event."
>
> Thursday was the Andrews' seventh wedding anniversary.

Let's stop here, for now. The last line is the punchline. The story can legitimately stop here and achieve good effect. But the writer may elect to wrap-up some obvious odds and ends by continuing:

> Postmaster Oscar Farlane could only offer apologies. "When you handle millions of pieces of mail, an occasional mix-up is bound to occur.
> "I can only guess that the letter was somehow misplaced in some small cranny. An employee may have stumbled across it last week and placed it in our delivery system."

By continuing, the writer gave postal authorities the opportunity to explain the error and to shed light on the mystery.

In both options, the body *of* the story is related in the order of occurrence of events—chronological order. If you closely examine the story, you will find little if any material that can be deleted without greatly weakening the story or making it senseless.

Endings

The bright ending is as important as the lead. While the lead lures the readers into the story and sets up the ending, the ending is the ultimate point of interest for the reader.

The bright ending may take one of these forms:

The punchline ending, which satisfies reader curiosity by providing the information carefully withheld from the reader.

The un-ending, which leaves readers scratching their heads in puzzlement by purposely neglecting to reveal answers, or by revealing that there is no available conclusion.

Punchline Ending. The endings of brights used as examples previously are all punchline endings. The punchline is the favorite form for the feature writer.

Just as a comedian will rely on timing and delivery to milk maximum effect from a joke punchline, the feature writer carefully sets up (times) the punchline ending of a bright, then seeks to deliver that ending in the most effective manner.

While, in most features, the writer seeks a "natural" ending, the ending for a bright is so important that it must be manufactured. The entire bright is carefully arranged to support that ending. In other forms, the ending is merely a finishing touch to the overall story.

In the wedding card story, the punchline ending was short, crisp and to the point:

> Thursday was the Andrew's seventh wedding anniversary, an ironic coincidence in the delivery of a seven-year-old wedding card.

The writer avoided the greatest temptation: to over-write or over-elaborate the punchline ending.

The ending is so important that the writer may understandably feel an urge to underscore it.

Very few readers could miss the irony, even if the writer neglects to tell them that it's ironic.

As Senator Sam Ervin once said, you can draw a picture of a horse, or you can draw a picture of a horse and label it "horse."

The Un-ending. Although somewhat rare, some brights lend themselves to the un-endings. The reader may feel as though he has been "had," yet most readers may take this with a good-natured chuckle.

The un-ending, like the punchline ending, is crisp and to the point. Here is an example:

> The meter maid walked around the brown mare slowly, scratched her head, then wrote out a parking ticket.
>
> The horse was hitched to a downtown parking meter this morning and, in obvious violation of the law, stood on the sidewalk.
>
> Not to be stymied by the lack of vehicle license tag, meter maid Sandra Allen scribbled "Brown Mare" under the vehicle description heading, and "0" under license number.
>
> Mrs. Allen placed the citation in the horse's saddle and left.
>
> When she returned, an hour later, the horse was gone but the ticket remained. It was taped to the meter with this note:
>
> "I will mail you a silver bullet to pay the fine."
>
> It was signed: "The Lone Ranger."

This qualifies as an "un-ending" because it emphasized a key, unanswered question: who was that rider, anyhow?

SUMMARY

A front page story always provides a lift for a reporter, even when the story is a short bright without a by-line. The bright gives the reporter an opportunity to cash in on the little oddities of life.

Although a bright is short and very terse, talented and sometimes difficult writing is required—a special, valuable knack to capture these small oddities effectively in few words.

EXERCISES

Part One
1. Clip a bright from the local newspaper. Determine which structural form is used. Then rewrite it to fit it into a different structural form.
2. Using that clipping, determine whether the bright could be enlarged into a full-sized human interest or news feature by adding detail and description.

Part Two
1. Write a bright from the following information:

At a University homecoming-eve rally, a hat was stolen. The student who snatched the hat for a souvenir was quickly apprehended by police Detective Roland Summers. According to the police offense report, the hat was a "blue police service hat with a badge attached that had a colonel's insignia." The hat belonged to Police Chief Arnold Dodge who was standing around by the bonfire when the student grabbed the hat. The student William D. Rose, 20, of Cranford Hall, room 211, was charged with petit larceny. "There was no way I was going to let the guy get away," Summers said. "My job was at stake."
2. Using a different bright structure, rewrite it.

10   Sidebars

When the forces of nature are unleashed in the terrible form of a tornado, hurricane or flood, even the most experienced reporter may feel somehow incapable of *really* communicating the awe of the disaster to his readers.

The loss of lives and property become sad but inadequate statistics in the page-one, lead news story that proclaims the disaster and, in the coolly impersonal professionalism of hard newswriting, reduces each of the thousands of individual human tragedies by the common statistical denominator.

This ficticious news story cannot do the real job of communicating the disaster because of format limitations inherent in a news story:

> (headline) Tornado Levels Alabama Town
>
> McMann, Ala.—A half-mile wide tornado roared through the heart of this North Alabama town of 12,000 people at 8 p.m. Wednesday, killing 23, injuring 341, and leveling half the structures within city limits.
>
> Civil Defense officials estimate damage at $50 million.
>
> Hundreds of citizens saw the black, funnel cloud touch down a mile west of the city limits. The twister then swept eastward through the central business district and the dense residential section east of town.

The story would continue its matter-of-fact account with reports from nearby hospitals, law enforcement officials, the governor's office, American Red Cross, the National Guard, and other sources of aid to victims which can provide information on the extent of the disaster.

But, in the account, people are statistics. The reporter must then look for another means of communicating the disaster: a sidebar feature story.

A sidebar feature is a normally brief account that relates directly to a major news story or in-depth story on the same page or, at least, in the same edition.

In the fictitious tornado coverage, the reporter may use a sidebar approach to supplement the hard news story by communicating in terms of people:

As the howling black funnel devoured houses a block away, Charles Adams muttered a brief prayer and herded his sobbing wife and children into the basement.

From beneath piled mattresses, they could hear the roar of destruction coming closer and closer. They felt the vibrations of their wind-battered home.

Then, they heard the roar fade.

"Dear Lord, thank you," Adams recalled saying as he cautiously emerged from the basement and breathed a sigh of relief as he saw that his house was reasonably intact.

Then he looked around and gasped. Every other house within a three-block radius was reduced to a pile of rubble.

"I felt so relieved and so awfully sad at the same time," Adams said. "My neighbors were good people. All I could do was to start digging through the rubble. I just knew everyone was dead."

Perhaps miraculously, hundreds of people emerged, dazed, from basements and rooms in the center of the houses.

"After a minute or two, they would come out of the shock and pitch-in to help save other neighbors," Adams said. "You never saw people work so hard. We went through that rubble furiously. It was a chance to rob that tornado of some of its victims."

About 15 minutes after the tornado passed, the first fire truck fought its way through blocked streets to reach Adams' neighborhood. A police cruiser quickly followed.

"When firemen and police got here, they did everything they could to help," Adams said. "Two firemen and a policeman were injured, cut by the broken glass, but they refused to quit."

Adams kicked a pile of broken roofing tile and waved his arm over the destruction.

"Most of the neighbors were like me," he said. "They worked darned hard to earn a living. Almost every penny you make goes into your property, your home.

"If that twister had hit my home, everything that I had worked 20 years for would have been destroyed. That's what happened to my neighbors, they got out alive, and that's all."

Adams shared one loss with his neighbors. The McMann Textile Co., which employed most men in the town, was destroyed.

"The ironic thing about it is that I could lose my house after all," Adams said. "I'm out of a job, so I can't make my payments.

"But, after this, I'm not worried. The Lord will provide."

Without the sidebar, readers across the nation would have missed the real story of the tornado: human disaster, faith, courage and strength.

While a reader can hardly empathize with cold statistics, he can readily empathize with fellow humans who are captured, in print, facing great loss with courage.

Some critics charge that journalists, in writing such stories, simply exploit human suffering for a by-line ego trip. Yet, because of such stories, people are often so moved that they contribute money, food and clothing to help those people in need.

Types of Sidebars

Not all sidebars deal with disasters. Many other types of sidebars are designed to illuminate the impact or significance of news stories by providing an outlet for the often relevant information that won't fit into the normal, hard news structure.

Personality Sketch

The personality sketch often accompanies major news stories in which a new public figure has just grabbed the public limelight.

If, in a city election, a "darkhorse" candidate wins the mayoral race, the city hall reporter may use the personality sketch as a means of introducing the new mayor to his readers. The personality sketch would accompany the election returns story:

"Now, we're going to clean up this town," Mayor-elect George C. Petroff declared as final vote returns were posted, giving him a 200-vote edge over his closest competitor Lew Jacobs.

If Petroff, 44, was as surprised by his victory as other politicians were, he didn't reveal it in his ho-hum smile, nor his confident "I'll win, don't worry" comment when he trailed earlier by 189 votes.

"Look around you, it's easy to see why I won," he said. "We've had four major police corruption scandals this year, two city hall officials were convicted of accepting bribes, and so many cases of conflict of interest can be found in city government that no one has bothered to list them all."

Petroff's fiery blue eyes glowed as he relished the job ahead. As an assistant district attorney, he was fired last year for "insubordination" after refusing to drop bribery charges against the two officials who were later convicted.

"George Petroff is honest and he is a fighter," a high city official said after the election. "I only question whether he has the intelligence to do the job he is undertaking."

Petroff became an attorney five years ago after spending 18 years on the police force and rising to a captaincy. As a policeman, he was wounded twice in gunbattles which, boards of inquiry found, may have been avoided.

In 1968, Petroff was wounded in the chest when he led a police charge on a house where a gunman was holding out.

In 1963, he was shot in the left leg when he refused to drop his gun after a burglar approached him from behind. He still limps slightly because of that wound.

"George will always be, basically, a hard-nosed, honest cop," said Mrs. Margie Petroff, his wife of 25 years. "And, right now, this city needs a hard-nosed, honest cop as mayor."

The personality sketch is not an attempt at a major, in-depth "word-portrait" of the subject. As a sidebar, a much shorter format is needed so that the story may be fitted on the same page with the news story.

In the above example, the writer merely outlines the main elements of interest about the mayor-elect so that the reader may perceive the nature of the man who has been elected mayor.

Empathy Sidebars

The empathy sidebar seeks to catch the impact of a hard news story by using a human example or by seeking out a human viewpoint of the event.

The term "sob story" evolved from this type of feature writing. Some reporters are so talented in this specialty that they may boast, with justification, that they can get anyone to tell them anything.

While the writing may be sometimes difficult, the reporting is often a challenge for any journalist's resourcefulness.

A vigil story is a common variation. After an airplane that carried a college football team crashed, a midwestern newspaper sent one reporter to the scene and another to the home of a local athlete who played on that team.

At the home, the reporter uncomfortably waited for news of the young man in the living room with his parents. The reporter was a family friend, and this made the vigil even worse for him. Yet, he wrote the story professionally: a sidebar story on the vigil.

Police beat reporters sometimes inherit the unhappy responsibility of writing sidebar stories on families of murder or accident victims. Or, for a different twist, a courts beat reporter may write a story on the mother of a convicted murderer.

Not all empathy sidebars have unhappy endings, however. When a schoolbus carrying a high school band overturned, a reporter gloomily rushed to the house of parents for a vigil story. The telephone rang and, when the father answered, everyone watched his face with dread.

Then tears came to the father's eyes—tears of joy. His son was calling to say that no one was seriously hurt, despite initial reports of "several serious injuries." The reporter was almost as relieved as the family.

Reaction Sidebars

People are often more interested in what other "common folks" say and think, than they are in what expert news analysts have to say. This tendency may be seen in readership surveys which, almost invariably, show that letters to the editors are much more frequently read than the stately, well-written editorials and columnists' commentaries.

Whenever an event of major public interest takes place, many newspapers send out reporters to sample public reaction.

When ill-fated Apollo 13 limped back to earth after an abortive attempt to reach the moon, The Dayton *Daily News* sent reporters to appliance sections of major stores to catch reactions of citizens who stood around floor-model television sets, watching and praying for the astronauts' safe recovery.

As it became evident that the men were safe, cheers and applause broke out, and strangers smiled happily at each other for a fleeting moment.

The reporters quickly gathered comments and reactions, then returned to the newsroom to quickly assemble them into a reaction sidebar.

An unusual single viewpoint may provide the source of reaction needed for a reaction sidebar.

Perhaps a presidential candidate is in town to speak from the courthouse steps. The substance of his speech is being well-covered by a multitude of newsmen.

One imaginative newsman decides on a different approach: he finds a 100-year-old man who actively belongs to the candidate's party. The old timer has, in his years, attended such rallies given by 15 presidential candidates, seven of whom were elected President. The political observer's comparisons of candidates and his reaction to the new-comer, is a natural story.

The Mood Sidebar

Through delicate and sensitive writing, a reporter may success-fully capture the impact of an event or situation by observing and reporting the often subtle signs of the prevalent mood of people involved.

The mood piece attempts to do with words what an artistic photographer can do with pictures. In the aftermath of a disaster, a newspaper or news magazine may carry a photo spread that profoundly catches the mood by focusing on disaster-dulled eyes, silhouettes of hapless victims kicking through debris, or highly shadowed photos of one human being comforting another.

Unlike the empathy sidebar, the mood piece makes no attempt to focus on specific viewpoints or experiences. The writer may purposely seek a "slightly out of focus" effect—a dream-like (or nightmarish) walk through a profound human experience.

McMann, Ala.—

The elderly woman softly hummed "A Mighty Fortress" as she busily swept her kitchen floor.

The house was gone and only the floors remained somehow in-tact in the aftermath of yesterday's tornado.

Two blocks away, a young girl sobbed and cried, "Tramp, Tramp, here boy, Tramp, Tramp."

Nothing stirred in the 12-foot pile of rubble that was once her home.

On Newton Drive, residents who lived on the south side of the roadway sat on front steps, in separate family units, and stared with lingering terror across the street.

The north side of the street was decimated.

"Mommy, daddy. can we go home now?" a small girl whim-pered as her family stood silently before the foundation of a house

"We are home, honey," her mother whispered.

Some major streets in the 28-block tornado-stricken area were cleared early today so that emergency vehicles could gain access to victims.

By 11 a.m., the open roads were jammed with traffic as curi-ous on-lookers from nearby cities swarmed through shaking their heads in awe.

"They're like vultures," an old man said bitterly. "We should sell popcorn and soft drinks and charge admission. We could get enough money that way to rebuild the town."

Even 15 hours after the funnel cloud roared through, an occa-sional siren wailed as still another injured victim was pulled from the rubble.

At Central High School gymnasium, which escaped with minor damage, the American Red Cross distributed food and clothing to the thousands who had lost everything.

"No, we aren't going to take charity," a man declared angrily as he eyed the long line of people waiting to enter the gym.

"We can't be bull-headed now, Robert," his wife said. "The children need food and clothes. Do you know of any other way? Let's get in line."

At Mercy Hospital, sick and injured people lay on mattresses that had been placed in hallways, reception rooms, and almost anywhere else where there is space for one.

"The entire staff has been working straight through since the first ambulances came in," a nurse said. "Our doctors are ready to drop on their feet."

Another stretcher came in and the bearers had to carefully step around and over patients on floor mattresses.

Two hours later, the elderly woman had stopped sweeping the kitchen floor.

She stood, leaning against her broom, immobile.

"Grandma, please come with us," a young woman said. "It will be better tomorrow."

"Nothing will ever be the same again," the old woman said as she sat on the floor and sobbed.

In this story, the reporter considered identification of the victims unimportant. He wanted the readers to perceive the story as a whole, not as a collection of individual viewpoints.

PURPOSES OF A SIDEBAR

No other type of feature story has as serious a mission as the sidebar feature.

While other features seek, primarily, to entertain the readers, the sidebar is a major informational tool that enables the newsman to fully inform the readers. The purposes of a sidebar feature are:

To illuminate the impact and significance of a hard news story.

As noted earlier, events or disasters of great magnitude can be so awesome that readers cannot fully comprehend the true impact from traditional hard news accounts.

While the hard news story *tells* the readers about the event, the sidebar *shows* readers the event.

To humanize the news and enable readers to identify with those people involved in the event.

In the tornado story examples, the plight of individual human beings was carefully depicted so that each reader could feel sympathy, not for a statistic, but for another human being.

As a device to give vital information that would not normally fit into the format of a hard news story.

Remember the scene at the hospital? In the hard news format, the hospital situation would be treated like this:

> Some 471 patients crowded into the 200-capacity Mercy Hospital.

Although the news account is concise and accurate, it misses the *real* situation: stretcher bearers stepping over patients who were lying everywhere on mattresses.

FINDING A SIDEBAR

At the scene of any major news event, an alert reporter can see several sidebar possibilities within minutes after arriving.

Whenever people are gathered to share a major experience, all the material a reporter needs for a sidebar is present. Only the reporter's technique in extracting information may vary.

Let's examine such approaches by performing sidebar coverage at a major political rally during a heated gubernatorial campaign.

You accompany the veteran political reporter to the rally. He has been assigned "hard news" coverage of the speech, while you are expected to write a sidebar feature.

Within moments after arriving at the county counthouse steps, from which the candidate will speak, you consider the first sidebar possibility:

The Overview Approach

In this the reporter concentrates on capturing the crowd as a collective personality, and he also shows how that crowd reacts under the stimulus of the speech.

In this case, the overview approach meets with all the necessary ingredients: a lively, interesting crowd; a colorful setting; and a fascinating stimulus (the candidate).

The gubernatorial candidate is a legendary campaign figure in the state. An outspoken populist, he is among the last of the politicians to still shed coat and tie and roll up his shirt sleeves to exhort the crowd.

Before the speech, a country-western music band merrily plays "Bluegrass" music to warm up the crowd for the candidate.

Most crowd members clap their hands in tempo with the music, and a few grab partners to dance along.

In the hot, Southern sun, a campaign aide mops his brow and teases the crowd to a greater pitch of anticipation by extolling the virtues of the candidate. When the candidate finally appears, the crowd has been primed to ecstacy.

Busily jotting down observations just in case you decide to use this approach, you continue to be alert to other sidebar possibilities:

The Human Viewpoint

In this approach the reporter focuses his sidebar through the eyes of one or a few select individuals.

Standing a few feet from the reporter, a middle-aged farmer stuffed his hands into coverall pockets and stared at the candidate without emotion. His weather-tanned face; straight, wiry body, and wizened eyes hinted at a character which may fascinate the readers through his viewpoint.

Close by, a small boy clutched a bumper-sticker bearing the candidate's name. He listened to his hero with an awed expression.

At the fringe of the crowd, two men stood wearing coats and neckties. They did not applaud with the crowd, nor laugh at the candidate's jokes. It was obvious that they were there to observe and not to support the candidate.

In each case, you, the reporter, has a potentially unique viewpoint within the crowd which can be used to tell your story.

The Supporting Cast

Behind the scenes of any major event, scores of people must work to provide services that are needed by others. These members of the supporting cast can often provide unique viewpoints of the event.

Standing a dozen paces from the candidate, Capitol City Police Sergeant Joe Brooks nervously eyes the crowd and frequently lifts a portable radio to re-position officers in the crowd. Sgt. Brooks has provided police protection for each candidate who has spoken in the city.

During the speech, a "heckler" stands to "bait" the candidate with an unfriendly question. The candidate quickly responds to the question so effectively that the heckler is left speechless. As a reporter, you recognize the heckler as a political functionary for another candidate.

Slipping through the crowd, the candidate's campaign manager listens not to the speech, but to the crowd reaction. He eyes the composition of the crowd and sensitively tries to gauge the support for each point made by the candidate.

Campaign workers push through the crowd, handing out pamphlets, bumper-stickers and buttons. An attractive college girl cajoles smiles of acceptance from reluctant crowd members who earlier rejected pamphlets from male campaign workers.

Any or all of these people could easily provide a lively sidebar angle for the reporter.

Ironies and Oddities Approach

Contradictions and contrasts are always of interest to people. When something out of the ordinary is present, then the reporter's sidebar assignment becomes easy.

While the candidate extolls law and order, his speech is interrupted by the sounds of gunfire as police subdue two would-be bank robbers a half a block from the courthouse. The driver of the get-away car, which is stopped by police gunfire, runs into the crowd where he is captured by the candidate's supporters.

The campaign workers learn, after handing out hundreds of pamphlets, that the name of the candidate has been misspelled on the covers. Quality education is a major campaign item for the candidate.

The candidate's opponent walks through the crowd, shaking the hands of startled voters.

Summary of Approaches

These are only a few of scores of possible approaches. Each type of event will provide other possible approaches or variations of those which have been mentioned.

The basic ingredient is the "human animal" and the amusing, sometimes strange, behavior of that creature. By following his curiosity and by being observant, a reporter is never at a loss for material. His only real problem is deciding which, of all the possible approaches, is best for his story.

WRITING A SIDEBAR

In writing a sidebar, the reporter must be aware of the peculiar nature of this feature form and of the purposes which it must serve.

The sidebar will, essentially, ride the coattails of the main news story to get page-one prominence. This great advantage results in some format limitations:

It must be fairly brief so that it can be placed alongside the main story. Page one space is a critical commodity. Even the most glittering feature story must take secondary priority to major news stories that battle for front page position.

If the sidebar is fairly long, then the copy desk is faced with these unattractive alternatives:

Donate a large share of page one to coverage of one event. Between the main story and the long sidebar, little space would remain for other items.

Jump the sidebar to the inside pages after a few paragraphs. The great disadvantage is that most readers simply stop reading when the story breaks with the bold-faced words: "Continued on page 10."

Place the entire sidebar on an inside page and promote the story by inserting a notice: "See page 10 for a related story" in the middle of the main story. The disadvantage is that most of the coattail effect is lost.

The reporter must include a general reference to the nature of the event, even though it may be redundant when coupled with information given in the main news story. Strangely, some readers will read the sidebar without reading the main news story. This means that, in order to understand the sidebar, the reader must have a brief summary paragraph, high in the story, about the news aspect.

In the tornado story examples, the writer carefully summarized the news aspects in the initial example. Yet, in the mood piece, the reader who had missed the main news story would only know that a tornado struck a large area of McMann, Ala. yesterday, causing great destruction.

The reporter must make the decision concerning inclusion of background by considering the effect of various degrees of backgrounding on the overall story.

In the mood piece, too much summary would have detracted from a feature style that is purposely unspecific and sketchy. When a writer purposely avoids identifying people within the story, it seems hardly logical to spoil the effect by inserting such a glut of specific information as:

> The half-mile wide twister ripped through the heart of this North Alabama town at 8 p.m. Wednesday, killing 23, injuring 341, and levelling half the structures within the city.

Besides the format limitations, the reporter must be aware of the purposes of the sidebar feature, and he must emphasize the strengths inherent in such a form:

Concentrate on mood, description, and detail. Few reporters would miss such an opportunity to display their writing talents.

After struggling to achieve a calm, professional detachment in writing the hard news version, the reporter may emerse himself in the creativity of feature writing—a different world in which statistics become human beings.

All of the "frills" which he struggled to omit from the hard news stories are now his tools in constructing the sidebar.

Because of this sudden change of perspective, reporters must often battle the urge to overwrite, to become emotionally caught up in the descriptions, mood and detail to the point that objectivity is brushed aside. Yet, a professional journalist knows that the sidebar requires the same strict adherence to professionalism in accurate, non-opinionated reporting, as any other form of news or feature writing.

To avoid overwriting, the reporter must limit inclusion of material to that which he saw, heard or smelled—and never use that which he thought or inferred.

Emphasize points which give readers a chance to psychologically identify with people involved with the event.

The individual viewpoints of the event as told by witnesses or survivors are integral parts of any sidebar story. If a tragedy has occurred, then these individual accounts, in the victim's own words, allow readers to see themselves in similar circumstances.

SUMMARY

In researching and writing sidebar features, the reporter may often alternately wear two hats: that of the veteran newsman, and that of the sensitive feature writer.

To the reader, who sees the same reporter's by-line over both the cold, hard news account, and over the sensitive, delicate feature story, the journalist who manages to write both accounts must seem like a schizophrenic. In one story, the journalist has rattled off aweful statistics with the impersonal coolness of a computer; and, in the other story, he wrote with such obvious sensitivity that even the most hard-bitten city editor may have shed a tear or two.

The reporter must, of course, have both of these characteristics; sensitivity and calm detachment, to perform his demanding job. The sidebar feature is often an ultimate test of both.

EXERCISES

1. Clip a major news story from your local newspaper. Study the story and determine a possible sidebar approach. How would you research the sidebar? What additional information would be revealed through the sidebar to inform your readers of the significance of the event?

2. Clip a sidebar feature from the newspaper and the news story that it accompanies. What purpose did the sidebar serve? Did it divulge information that otherwise would have been missed by the readers? Did it help you to understand the event more fully?

11 Color Stories

A color story assignment can draw out a child-like quality in even the most grizzled veteran reporter. Instead of facing the dismal prospect of wading through debris and talking to victims of a tornado, the reporter joins a happy sports crowd, watches a parade or cavorts in a large, public festival.

A color story, by definition, is a light, descriptive feature that captures the mood and atmosphere of a festive event. It can either be a self-contained single story or a sidebar.

If the World Series is to be played in a nearby city, reporters may eagerly suggest color story coverage to gain a free press pass which entitles the holder to a prime seat in the auxiliary press section.

The reporter who undertakes the coverage begins his work even before reaching the stadium.

"Tickets, tickets," a tall man yells as he holds up a dozen World Series tickets.

"How much?" the reporter asks.

"Just $20 each," he replies.

After identifying himself, the reporter learns that the ticket "scalper" has done a brisk trade in selling the tickets which cost $10 when sold by the ballpark. With all tickets sold, however, the scalpers were getting up to $50 for each ticket.

It's an election year and several politicians are taking advantage of the large crowd to gain public exposure. On one key pedestrian overpass which carried many baseball fans to the park, two gubernatorial candidates, a U.S. Senate candidate, and an incumbent U.S. Congressman stood to shake hands with prospective voters.

"I'm not going to vote for any of those guys," a disgruntled fan griped. "Imagine, exploiting a World Series game to politick!"

Inside the stadium, people swarmed around food stands, drifted toward their seats, then looked frantically for the seat numbers that corresponded with those on their tickets.

CATEGORIES OF RESOURCES

While sizing up the normal sports crowd chaos, the reporter quickly takes inventory of the resources available to him in gathering material. Basically, these resources can be divided into three categories:

1. People, both in the crowd and in the supporting cast.
2. The attraction, the common thread of interest that unites the people.
3. The reporter's sensory perceptions. What does he see, hear, smell and feel (and *not* what does he think)?

In this particular feature story assignment, the reporter will try to supplement the game coverage with a story that is so descriptive and lively that the reader will have the impression that he is sitting in the stadium.

A ready market certainly exists for such coverage. Even though television allows a sports fan to watch the game from a better viewpoint (with expert commentary and instant replays), from the comfort of his living room, most fans would instantly pay $10 for a seat behind a stadium post for the pleasure of attending the game in person.

Why?

Probably two factors can help explain this strange quirk of human nature. First, the television cameras are focused on the ball and not the crowd. Even the most avid fan often enjoys the antics of fellow humans in the crowd as much as he enjoys the game itself.

Secondly, to attend such a game is often a childhood dream. Although children grow up, dreams linger. Even the most sophisticated adults sometimes enjoy the status of attending a dream event such as a World Series.

The reporter is no different from any other sports fan, except that he is paid to fulfill the childhood dream and to enjoy the antics of the crowd.

The informational resource of interesting people is abundant at the stadium:

The supporting cast of hotdog hawkers, guards, janitors and ushers is busily struggling to accommodate the demands of the crowd.

Children, always a prime resource, are everywhere, squirming with excitement.

Elderly people, with their unique points of perspective, are scattered through the crowd, awaiting the first pitch with practiced patience.

A large variety of the more eccentric specimens of the human race are running about.

The second resource, the point of attraction, is very strong. The baseball players on each team are obviously keyed up. Tension is in the air as every spectator casts nervous glances toward the playing field.

Stimuli to the reporter's senses are everywhere to meet the requirements of the third research resource. Colorful banners and clothing are scattered through the crowd. The bright green artificial turf with geometric white lines and the white and gray players' uniforms catch the reporter's eye. The aroma of hotdogs, popcorn and peanuts hangs everywhere. The jabber of the excited crowd builds into a steady crescendo as game time approaches. The soft crunch of wrappers and the sticky or slippery feel of spilled liquids under foot are traditional "feelings" at a ballgame.

With the first pitch still a long time away, the reporter decides to gather objective, sensory perceptions. Using his press pass, he walks onto the field before the players emerge from the locker rooms for pregame field practice.

Standing on the pitcher's mound with the excitement of a small boy, the reporter slowly turns around to look at the stands through the eyes of the starting pitcher. He sees a sea of white shirts, sprinkled with red, yellow and blue, making eddies toward the hotdog stands and pouring into streams down the aisles. The field, which looks so large from the stands, loses its Olympian proportions on ground level. Even the distant center field fence appears to be an easy lob away.

The weather also provides an impression. The muggy humidity and the breeze off the nearby river combine for a nippy, cloudy autumn afternoon. Pennant flags that represent each major league baseball team flap in the wind.

Leaving the playing field, the reporter decides to chat with members of the supporting cast. He sees a middle-aged usher who has a friendly smile and an air of excitement about him. The reporter asks for his impressions of the crowd.

"No, this isn't like the crowds we get during regular season," he said. "This is my sixth World Series as an usher. Always, there are lots of people here who don't know anything about the game, they just come for the prestige.

"Now, see that woman over there with the fur coat? She doesn't even know who's playing—she had to ask me. Yeah,

I get excited about the Series games, I'd be lying if I didn't say so. I've watched every home game this year, so I'm a real rabid fan. I'll get to watch a lot of the game after everyone gets settled into their seats."

Drifting further through the crowd, the reporter sees a police sergeant standing near a hotdog stand, watching the crowd walk by.

"I wish that I could watch the game, but you can bet that I'll be too busy to see it," he said. "Whenever you get 55,000 people together, a small percentage of them will be troublemakers who won't have any consideration for other people.

"Two years ago when the Series was played here before, we arrested 33 people for everything ranging from public intoxication to assault with a deadly weapon.

"Most people are really nice, though. Kids are always coming by, between innings, to talk with me. Last time, a little old lady bought me a cup of coffee. She said I looked really tired. I didn't have the heart to tell her I had just finished a cup."

A young man walked by carrying a tray of softdrinks.

"Yeah, the sales are real good," he said. "People seem like they're in a spending mood when they come to the Series. During regular games, a guy may try to economize a little, but during the Series it seems like they do everything up big like it's a special event.

"No, I don't care anything about the game. I'd like to see the Reds win so the customers would be happy, but I don't like baseball. It's too slow, football is my game."

At a refreshment stand, a young woman busily slapped hotdogs into buns while glancing nervously at the machine where a score of weiners were cooking.

"This is just a job to me," she said. "It's not much fun, either. People are always in such a hurry. They get so impatient. If they don't get service right away, they cuss at you and slam down their money."

As the stands begin to fill, the reporter begins to scan the people for interesting-looking characters.

An elderly woman hobbles by, wearing a Cincinnati Reds baseball cap. She is carrying a first baseman's mit in one hand and a pennant in the other.

"I'm 86-years-old today, and this is the first baseball game I've ever been too. I've watched lots of them on television, so my grandchildren are treating me today.

"The glove? Anybody who would sit behind third base without a glove has got to be nuts. Have you ever seen any of them line-drive fouls? It's enough to kill you if you got hit in the head. I intend to reach 100, so I'm not taking any chances.

"Sure, I'm rooting for the Reds. But I've got $10 riding on Oakland. The Reds don't have the pitching depth that Oakland has. You can't win if you can't hit the ball, and nobody has hit Oakland's pitching this year."

The game begins and the crowd settles down to watch. The reporter listens to the shouts of the fans:

"Hey ump, you got dust in your eyes?"

"Come on, get the ball over the plate."

"You idiot! Keep running!"

"Ya got a hole in ya bat?"

"He was safe a mile!"

"Foul ball? Ump, you're the only foul ball I see."

Walking slowly around the stadium, with one eye cocked onto the playing field, the reporter searches for more interesting people. He sees a young boy staring at the field as if he were in a trance.

"We came all the way from Akron," he said. "Daddy promised that if I hit .300 this year in Little League, he'd take me to the World Series if it was played in the Midwest. I hit a .321 average, so here we are.

"I'm a catcher, so I'm watching Johnny Bench because he's the best."

As if on a cue, the runner on first base scrambled toward second base in a steal attempt. Bench scooped up a low pitch, straightened and threw a blistering peg to the second baseman. The runner was called out.

"See what I mean," the boy said happily. "He's got the quickest release I've ever seen. Nobody steals on Johnny."

In a box seat behind the home team's dugout, the reporter sees the woman, bedecked in a fur coat, who had asked the usher for the names of the teams who were playing.

"I was only kidding him," the woman said, laughing. "Believe me, I know all about the game. My husband is Neal Sommers, the pitcher. All I've heard for eight months, since Spring training, has been baseball.

"Sure, I'm nervous. Since Neal is a relief pitcher, I never know when he's going to play. During the regular season, if he has a good game, he's the best husband in the world. But if he is bombed out, then it's like living with a bear.

"With the series, it will be 10 times as good or bad, depending on what happens. Believe me, the money is secondary. How would you like to live with a World Series losing pitcher for a whole winter? I shudder to even think about it."

As the game progresses, Sommers enters briefly as a relief pitcher, throws 12 pitches, and leaves the game. Of the 12 pitches, five are walloped by the batters for hits, including a homerun.

As the game ends and the disappointed fans storm out of the stadium, the reporter sees the 86-year-old woman. She is grinning broadly and clutching a souvenir baseball in her glove.

"What did I tell you?" she says happily. "Oakland won, and I got a line-drive foul."

"Tell the truth, grandma," a woman said.

"Well, all right. It wasn't a line drive, it was a pop-up."

CONSTRUCTING THE STORY

Returning to the newsroom, the reporter has ample material to construct his color story. As noted in the definition, a color story may be either a sidebar or a self-contained feature to stand alone on its own merits.

This World Series color story can be written either way.

Because the main event is a sports story, the reporter, who works for the "city desk," not the sports department, may write his story as a separate, page-one feature which would not be directly tied to the lead sports story: World Series coverage.

Or, he may write the color story as a sidebar to a page-one sports story on World Series coverage.

The decision of whether to write an inclusive, self-sufficient story, or a sidebar, must be made before the first word is typed because the formats are greatly different:

A color sidebar. This uses passing glimpses of the theme of the main event as a point of reference, while concentrating on off-beat viewpoints, people and description. The main focus is on the people who attend, and not on the event.

An inclusive color story. This wraps up the highlights of the main event in sufficient detail to inform readers of what happened, but still emphasizes the off-beat and unusual, and the peculiarities of the crowd.

The decision would probably be made by the news editor, who determines the content of page one. If he prefers to emphasize a straight account of the game, then the color story would be a sidebar to the main sports story that would begin on page one. If he preferred to keep all series sports coverage together on the sports pages, then he may want a self-contained, inclusive color story for page one.

Let's examine both options in relation to writing techniques:

The Color Sidebar

The lead of the sidebar color story may make only passing reference to the nature of the event, sometimes ignoring that overall nature all together, relegating such references to the body of the story.

The sidebar is positioned so that readers will probably read the main story as well, so there is no reason to dwell on the main event in the body of the story, much less the all-important lead.

Instead, the lead of the sidebar color story establishes the angle —the special viewpoint from which the reporter will give insight to the event.

Let's examine the World Series color sidebar for a couple of possible leads. The first example makes no reference to the event:

> Wearing her trusty first baseman's mit, 86-year-old Louise Wilson pulled the bill of her Cincinnati Reds' cap down over her bespectacled eyes to blot out the sun, then settled to wait on "them line-drive fouls."
>
> "Anybody who would sit behind third base without a glove has got to be nuts," she said, referring to the foul balls that sometimes shoot into crowds.

The second version, below, draws on the same character to establish the tone of the story, but works in a passing reference to the event:

> Despite the Cincinnati Reds' baseball cap perched jauntily atop her head, Mrs. Louise Wilson had "$10 riding on Oakland" when she attended her first World Series game ever, yesterday.
>
> Nine innings later, she left with a souvenir baseball, and a self-satisfied grin as Oakland won 5-4.

In neither version did the writer emphasize the event. Even in the second version, the colorful character of Mrs. Wilson received top billing. The game's outcome was given only "Oh, by the way . . ." mention.

The body of the color sidebar story follows the trend set by the lead. Any mention of the main event is made only as a point of perspective needed by the reader to understand the significance of the color material.

After introducing the young catcher from Akron, the reporter may write:

> "I'm a catcher, so I'm watching Johnny Bench because he's the best," he said.
> As if on cue, Bench scooped up a low pitch and threw a zinging peg to the second baseman who tagged out the baserunner who attempted to steal.

Prior to the insertion of the throw by Bench, no attempt had been made to recount the action of the ballgame. A single incident was plucked from game action and used *only* to reinforce the quotation of a young fan.

The writer may organize the body of the story by using "building blocks" of observations or characters. He may write several paragraphs about Mrs. Wilson, then write several more about the policeman, then the young fan, then the baseball pitcher's wife. He may arrange these blocks in descending order of reader interest to keep that technique of always giving the reader the most interesting material remaining so that the reader will continue to read the story.

Normally, a summary ending is used on color sidebars to wrap-up the event.

Feisty Mrs. Wilson could provide natural material for the ending:

> "What did I tell you?" Mrs. Wilson said jubilantly. "Oakland won and I got a line-drive foul."
> "Tell the truth, grandma," a woman said, grinning.
> "Well, all right. It wasn't a line drive, it was a pop-up."

The Inclusive Color Story

The lead of the inclusive color story must be a bit more informative than that of the color sidebar. It must make a strong reference to the event itself, while establishing the feature angle. A variation is to write a strong feature lead and use the second paragraph—the link—to quickly inform the reader about the event.

Let's examine these alternatives. The first example combines the feature angle with the strong reference to the event:

> Clutching a souvenir baseball, Mrs. Louise Wilson, 86, grinned triumphantly despite the 5-4 Cincinnati loss to the Oakland A's, which sent most Reds fans home muttering.

As you can see, the score took on much greater emphasis than in the color sidebar examples.

The second variation is, essentially, a two-paragraph lead:

"Sure, I'm rooting for the Reds, but I've got $10 riding on Oakland," Mrs. Louise Wilson, 86, declared as she settled into her seat. She was attending her first World Series game ever.

Mrs. Wilson proved to be a prophet as the Oakland A's out-slugged the Reds 5-4 to gain a one-game edge in the best of seven series, after a 4-run rally in the eighth inning.

Continuing with the body of the story, the writer uses the chronological highlights of the game as the backbone of the story, and fleshes out that backbone with color material. The body is written in straight, inverted pyramid style with a long, chronological sequence used to relate the progress of the game.

In the world Series example, the writer would introduce his characters in the order of their appearance in relation to the game.

The effect is similar to that of radio announcers broadcasting play-by-play accounts. In lulls between action, a "color man"—often a former player—provides amusing anecdotes and insight to entertain the listeners. Yet, the game itself is the main focus of interest.

SUMMARY

The color story is a delightful experience for both the reporter and the thousands who will read the story.

For the reporter, it is a welcome break—almost a paid vacation—after the exciting but exhausting chores of covering news stories and writing features about the more unpleasant aspects of life.

For the reader, the color story is a welcome island in a sea of serious, often threatening news and features about depressing subjects. The color story provides an opportunity for escapism, for a pleasant, although vicarious, experience.

And, in a tense world, who can begrudge a moment of fun for both the journalist and the reader?

EXERCISES

1. Using the World Series information, write a sidebar color story. The cast of characters;
   1. The old woman—Mrs. Louise Wilson, 86, of Louisville, Kentucky.
   2. Her daughter—Mrs. Barbara Holms, 58, of Cincinnati, Ohio.
   3. The young catcher—Andy Musso, 11, of Akron, Ohio.
   4. His father—Arnold Musso, 34, of Akron, Ohio.
   5. Fan who complains about politicking—Ralph Evans, 45, of Cincinnati, Ohio.

6. The usher—Paul McMillan, 60, of Cincinnati.
7. The policeman—Sergeant Samuel Burns, Cincinnati Police Department.
8. Softdrink vendor—Charles Bonner, 18, of Middletown, Ohio.
9. Woman hotdog seller—Wanda Powers, 20, of Hamilton, Ohio.
10. Pitcher Neal Sommers' wife—Susan Sommers, 25.
2. Using the same information, write an inclusive color story.
Below is an inning-by-inning summary of highlights:

First Inning:

Oakland at bat: Bert Campaneris hits a double. Doesn't score.

Cincinnati at bat: Joe Morgan singles, steals second base. Called out at home when trying to advance on a wild pitch.

Second Inning:

Oakland: A run is scored on a sacrifice fly after bases were loaded on two walks and an error.

Cincinnati: Johnny Bench doubles and Tony Perez homers. Cincinnati leads 2–1.

Third Inning:

Oakland: Reggie Jackson doubles. Reds Pitcher Don Gullett strikes out two batters to retire the side.

Cincinnati: Pitcher Vida Blue strikes out the side.

Fourth Inning:

Oakland: Vida Blue is hit by a pitched ball. Thrown out by Catcher Johnny Bench after taking large lead from first base. Perez, the first baseman, made the tag.

Cincinnati: Peter Rose singles, steals second, then scores on a double by Joe Morgan. Blue then retires the side. Reds lead 3–1.

Fifth Inning:

Oakland: With two outs, Joe Rudi hits line drive down right field line. Rose makes a diving catch to prevent an extra-base hit.

Cincinnati: Blue strikes out the side.

Sixth Inning:

Oakland: All three batters ground out.

Cincinnati: Dave Concepcion singles with two out.

Seventh Inning:

Oakland: After a walk to Campaneris, Gullet retires side.

Cincinnati: Bench hits home run with no runners on base. Score: Cincinnati 4, Oakland 1.

Eighth Inning:

Oakland: Reds replace Gullett with Sommers. First three batters single, then Jackson hits grand-slam homerun. The fifth batter doubles. Clay Carroll relieves Sommers, retires the side. Score: Oakland 5, Cincinnati 4.

Cincinnati: Oakland sends in Rollie Fingers in relief. After a single by Concepcion, Fingers retires the side.

Ninth Inning

Oakland: Carrol retires the side on two grounders and a strikeout.

Cincinnati: Rose hits ball over left-field fence, but umpire calls it foul. Rose then flies out, Morgan grounds out, and Bench flies out to deep center field to end game.

12   Personal Profiles

While a portrait is a succinct form of conveying an image, even the greatest artist is limited by his two-dimensional communications medium in capturing his subject on canvas. Leonardo Da Vinci did a masterful job of hinting at great character in his wonderful portrait of the Mona Lisa. Yet, Mona Lisa is imprisoned by the canvas.

She can't interact by speaking, walking in a certain manner, laughing a shrill laugh, or by biting her lower lip in a characteristic nervous mannerism. Her expression, great though it may be, is frozen forever.

A good writer can capture a character much better in print than a great artist can capture him on canvas. The writer can depict the subject from every conceivable angle, in every type of action, and catch the subtle characteristics that make the subject a unique human being.

Great authors are great descriptive writers. John Steinbeck's characters are so warm, alive and human that they become old, treasured friends to the readers. The pathetic brute, "Lenny," in *Of Mice and Men,* the wise, loving "Doc" of *Cannery Row* and the irrepressible "Danny" of *Tortilla Flat* are unforgettable to any Steinbeck reader.

Realizing the vast powers of the written word, the newspaper reporter must draw on all of his writing and reporting talents to undertake an in-depth, *Personal Profile* article.

By definition, a personal profile is an in-depth story on an individual that captures the essence of his personality, personal profile is the journalistic art of capturing a human being on paper.

The newspaper journalist faces two obstacles that neither the artist nor the author must contend with:

1. *The subject is a real human being* who may take heated issue with the reporter if the word-portrait in inaccurate or unflattering. While the artist may lose a fee if his subject is dissatisfied, his embarrassment is tempered by the fact that few people will see his substandard work.

If the reporter makes serious errors, then hundreds of thousands of readers will be exposed to them. Even worse, the subject may file a libel suit.

The author of fiction can hardly be criticized by the subjects who are figments of his imagination, much less face a libel suit from a ficticious character.

2. *The artist is limited by what he sees.* He makes no attempt to capture the whole person. The author of fiction is limited only by his imagination and talent, since he can use chapters and chapters to develop that character.

The newspaper journalist must try to capture that character within a reasonable amount of newspaper space. And he must not linger in developing interesting facets because the newspaper reader is an impatient soul who will quickly discard the article if it doesn't move along quickly.

A newspaper reporter has no time to elaborately set a stage for the introduction of a character. James Michener may leisurely, although effectively, use 100 pages to establish a proper setting before he introduces his first human character.

A newspaper journalist must immediately plunge into the character, grabbing the reader's interest by emphasizing a fascinating facet of the subject.

RESEARCH

Before writing the first word, the reporter may spend weeks of research, observing the subject from many viewpoints, talking to friends, enemies and colleagues. He may join the subject at the subject's home for a family dinner, scribbling notes between courses of the meal.

Frequently, a great deal of research is performed before the reporter even conceives the idea for a personal profile. A police reporter becomes well-acquainted with the police chief during day-to-day routine business. He has heard countless stories about the chief from other officers. He has seen the chief function under great pressure. He knows the peculiar quirks of character that makes the chief a unique human being.

Suddenly, one day, he sees the chief in a different light: a possible personal profile story.

The reporter is well-armed with observations and anecdotes gathered in past years on his beat. Yet, he knows that he has only seen the chief on his job, never at home with his wife and children. Even at his job, the reporter has never watched the chief tackle the routine mountain of paperwork that comes with administrative duties, nor watched him interact with his immediate staff members in the sanctity of his office, behind closed doors.

For several days, the reporter must "shadow" the chief in order to complete the picture of the *real* person who lurks behind the public image of a crusty, 60-year-old man who smiles before cameras and bellows at errant officers, city councilmen, and anyone else who dares to irritate him.

Although no reporter uses a checklist to guide him in his observations, the reporter must be alert to numerous characteristics. If a checklist were to be compiled, it would take this form:

Description of Physical Characteristics:

1. Facial Features. What features best give insight to the appearance? What features are distinguishing?

Does he has a fine, delicate face, or a craggy face with a long chin and beaked nose?

What is the color of his eyes? Their demeanor (sleepy, baady, probing, etc.)?

What characterizes his mouth? Is it wide, sensuous, thin, gaping?

Are his cheeks high, puffed, hollow or bony?

2. Complexion of skin. Is the texture chalky white, deep tan, chocolate, pale yellow, light brown?

3. Is his hair thick and oily, thinning, or receding?

What is the color? Is it shiny black? Carrot red?

What is the hair style? Moderate Afro, crew cut, parted in the middle and slicked down? Does he have facial hair?

4. What is his physical size?

How tall is he? How much does he weight?

How is that weight distributed?

Is he fit and muscular, or flabby?

5. What kind of clothing does he wear?

What colors does he prefer to wear? Does she tend to dress in dark basics, bright solids, or pastels?

Does he prefer a particular style? Does he wear suits with narrow lapels of yesteryear? Does she wear pants suits or mini-skirts?

Does he normally wear a hat? Is it a 10-gallon Texas-styled cowboy hat or a bowler? Does she wear a wide-brimmed hat of a style popular in the 1920s?

Does he normally wear a necktie? Is it wide or narrow, dark and plain, or bright plaid? Does he wear a bowtie?

What kind of shirt does he wear? A traditional white shirt or a brightly colored one? Does it have cufflinks?

Does she wear jewelry? Is that jewelry symbolic, such as a cross, or gaudy, such as a diamond necklace?

Does he wear eyeglasses or contact lens? If so, what kind?

What is the state of the clothing? Is it immaculate or somewhat rumpled?

What kind of socks or stockings does the subject wear? Does he wear white socks or formal men's stockings? Does she wear stockings? Are they tan or colored?

Are the shoes distinctive? Does he wear cowboy boots or wing-tipped shoes? Are they highly polished?

Are the clothes ill-fitting, perhaps indicating a change of weight or carelessness in shopping, or ar they tailor-fitted?

6. Habits and mannerisms can give character insight.

Does he smoke? How much? What kind of cigarette or pipe tobacco does he prefer? Does he smoke cigars or mild, filtered cigarettes? How does he hold it?

Does he have nervous ticks? Does he nod and jerk his head in a certain manner when he is nervous?

What does she do with her hands? Does she clasp them nervously, scribble, use them to describe as she talks?

What are his overall mannerisms? Does he squirm continuously, or sit placidly?

Does he drink liquor heavily?

Does he chew his lower lip or bite his fingernails?

7. Posture and bearing can play a role in image making.

Does he slouch in his chair or sit upright in a military manner? Are his shoulders hunched forward?

Does he walk with his head down, or with shoulders squared?

8. Voice and speech pattern often hint at character.

What is the voice tone? High and squeaky or low and gutteral?

Is the manner of speaking gruff or whining?

Does his volume tend to be loud or soft?

Is there a noticable accent, such as a Southern drawl?

What is the tone quality? Is it precise or gravelly?

How precise is his grammar? Does he speak in flawless grammar, normal conversational English, or does he misuse words, use slang, and use poor grammar?

What is his pace of speaking, fast, rhythmic, or slow? What is his style? Is he flowery, blunt or rambling?

9. What is the overall physical impression?

Does he resemble a famous person, such as John Wayne, W. C. Fields or Hubert Humphrey?

Does he appear to fit a classic occupational steretotype? Does the police chief look like the image of an Irish policeman?

What is his personality?

1. How does he express himself verbally?
   Is he gruff and salty?
   Does he speak obliquely, or come right to the point?
2. How energetic is he?
   Is he nervous or calm by nature?
   Is he aggressive or lethargic?
3. What is his temper?
   Does he rarely lose his temper?
   Does he have a "short fuse"?
4. How does he generally interact with others?
   Is he somewhat shy and reticent?
   Is he pushy or domineering?
5. Does he have a sense of humor?
   Is he fond of practical jokes?
   Does he enjoy off-color jokes?
   Does he often laugh at himself? At others?
6. Is he self-confident?
   Does he boldly proclaim his viewpoint, even when unpopular?
   Is he arrogant or meek?
7. Does his public image agree with his private character?
   Is he often grim and angry publicly, but good humored away from the public spotlight? Or visa versa?
8. How tenacious is he?
   Is he easily discouraged, or stubborn, perhaps bullheaded?
   Does he seem to enjoy battling long odds?

Evaluation of intelligence and ability to cope

1. How do colleagues, friends and enemies rate his professional competence?
   Is he considered brilliant or pedestrian?

Is he an example of the Peter Principle: the tendency to rise to a level of incompetence?

2. Away from the job, does he exhibit "common sense"?

Is he the type of genius who forgets to tie his shoelaces?

Can he carefully balance a city's budget, but leave his family budget in shambles?

Does his competence carry over to household chores?

3. Does he have a fine memory?

Can the politician remember the precinct-by-precinct vote breakdown from an election 10 years ago?

Does he have a photographic memory?

Does he have to write notes to himself to remember even major items? Does he usually lose the notes?

4. Does he have a professional instinct?

Does the policeman instinctively sense crime or danger?

Does the politician "feel" a subtle change in the mood of his constituency?

Background of the subject

1. Circumstances of birth: when, where and parents' names.
2. Dates and places where the subject lived.
3. Education.
4. Honors.
5. Name of spouse, date of marriage and names, ages of children.
6. Present residence. (Sometimes, a description is relevant).
7. Highlights of childhood.
8. Military service.
9. Religious affiliation and activities (if applicable).
10. Family accomplishments (example: a profile of a member of the Kennedy family would require at least a passing reference to the family's great deeds).
1. A chronological account of the subject's career.

Anecdotes and "insight" material

1. The subject tells amusing, informative or profound incidents and mileposts.
2. Friends and family members tell anecdotes about him.
3. Co-workers tell anecdotes, give observations.
4. Adversaries tell anecdotes and give observations.

Present status: what makes him of public interest?

1. What, exactly does he do? (title and explanation)
2. How does he do it?
3. How do others rate his performance?

4. What are the frustrations and rewards of the job?
5. Is he happy about his function?
6. Anecdotes about his job.

Dreams

1. Is he doing what he always wanted to do? If not, what was his original dream?
2. Is he ambitious? What are his ambitions?
3. Philosophically, what does he hope to accomplish in life?

Surroundings

1. What does his office look like?
   Does he have symbolic knick-knacks on his desk?
   Does he have pictures of his family?
   Is his office and desk cluttered or fastidiously neat?

Obviously, such a checklist would be impracticable for other than academic use for several good reasons:

1. A human being can hardly be defined by a standardized checklist form, which cannot possibly cover all or even most of the subtle characteristics that make the subject a unique person. Yet, at the same time, many of the items included would not be applicable to many, perhaps most, subjects.

2. Any attempt to formularize the study of the character that a reporter hopes to capture on paper would invariably lead to formularized writing. Each personal profile story must be written in a special style to effectively portray that person.

3. By faithfully following a checklist, the journalist would spend many unnecessary days gathering unusable detail which would not contribute an iota toward the purpose of the story.

Instead, think of the checklist as an illustration of the need to be organized an observant in your research. The small, often painfully subtle details may spell the difference between a superficial story and an effective word portrait.

Sometimes, the missing detail is overlooked for days before the reporter notices it. While researching for a profile on a respected police official, a reporter repeatedly returned to the subject's office to chat with him and search for that elusive key detail which he instinctively knew was missing.

During one such conversation, he noticed a photograph of a dignified minister with piercing eyes that seemed to stare over the subject's right shoulder from its position on top of a filing cabinet. It was a photograph of the man's father.

Mentioning the photograph, the reporter soon found himself scribbling notes frantically as the subject recalled his father's great influence on him. The father, he acknowledged, had established an achievement image that the subject had spent his life in seeking.

While the checklist hints broadly at such information, the reporter must go well beyond the surface to find the human being.

WRITING A PERSONAL PROFILE

After spending days with the subject, a reporter may fill several notebooks with quotations, anecdotes, observations and other information about almost every conceivable viewpoint from which the subject can be seen.

As noted in earlier chapters, organizing such voluminous material is an exhausting, sometimes tedious task of typing out notes, outlining the story, chopping, pasting, rewriting and rewriting.

With a personal profile, however, a delicate, artistic touch is a mandatory part of the task.

A reporter for The Dayton *Daily News* once spent weeks gathering material for an in-depth personal profile story on Don Crawford, the Dayton City Commission clerk, who was, years earlier, the first black to be elected to the City Commission. Retired from political office, Crawford still held great political influence.

After broaching the subject of writing a personal profile in a conversation with Crawford, the reporter interviewed him at length to start the research process.

Crawford was elected to the City Commission in 1961 and remained in office until 1967 when he suddenly quit to accept a city hall job.

"When I quit the commission, many people were disappointed in me," Crawford said. "They felt they were losing their champion in city hall. I was a symbolic creature. It wasn't easy for the casual observer to see that more often than not the vote was 4-1 or 3-2 against me. Crawford was a hero, but things weren't getting done. Now it's different, without the fanfare, commissioners pay more attention to me. The people probably have an advocate in a stronger position to help."

Crawford explained that his influence on commissioners is above board. "You do it simply by doing the job they hired you to do. They ask for my opinion and I give it to them."

During the interview, Crawford related how he reached his political apex. "I stumbled into Dayton, fell into Boy Scout work, and got pushed into the commission," he said. He was born in Clinton, Ky. on July 27, 1921. His father was a railroad chef. "We moved around a lot." He attended Kentucky State College. "I started into medicine, but my ego sidetracked me. Ever since I was a kid, I wanted to be one of the very best in whatever I did. I found out it would take a lot of money and probably some study in Europe to be one of the very best in medicine."

So Crawford settled for a career in scientific research, he said, receiving a bachelor of science degree in mathematics and physics. After graduating in 1942, he taught high school classes for a year, hoping to get an Army Air Corps commission during the war. When this didn't happen, he enlisted in the Navy, becoming one of the first black quartermasters.

After the war, he married his college sweetheart, Agatha, who was teaching in Dayton. "I came to pick her up here in April 1946. We thought we were going to Chicago to start life there, but I had to wait a few months for her to finish the term and I stumbled into Scouting." Crawford became district scout executive. By 1951, he was the assistant executive for the Miami Valley scout region. "What really sold me on scouting and Dayton was I found I could walk to the vice president's office at a place like NCR (National Cash Register) and get his time and attention because I was there on scouting. If Dayton was that kind of community with that kind of leadership, it deserved some looking into."

In 1961 the All Dayton Committee and black leaders decided it was time for a black city commissioner. They needed a black candidate with some appeal to white voters. "People at least knew Don Crawford and knew me as a Boy Scout leader, and that's a clean, healthy image to carry," he said.

Crawford said he didn't really want to get into politics and that he wasn't a member of any political group before the race. He did admit that C.J. McLin Sr., a powerful black politician, and his son "Mac Junior" were his friends. "Mac Senior had run for commission before, and he was terribly mistreated, even threatened. But he was always sure that a black could be elected. Long before I ever thought about running, he (Mac Senior) said, 'Someday, son, I predict you will be the first black city commissioner,'" Crawford said.

Crawford recalled that, perhaps because he wasn't expected to win, he didn't encounter much mud-slinging. "People were very decent to me all over town. They thought I had no chance. (Crawford chuckled at this latter observation).

"As late as 9 o'clock election night, some people pretended

to be friendly who were pleased to see me running fourth," he said. "The West Dayton votes came in later, however, and I jumped to a strong second. I received a fair vote in the rest of the city."

Crawford recalled that there were celebrations all over West Dayton, a predominately black area. "There was quite a celebration. Mac Senior literally cried because he was so overjoyed that his prediction was true."

After his election, Crawford recalled that the political situation for blacks changed considerably. "For years, the (Democratic) party would set up free hotdogs and beer on the West Side every election. Mac Junior finally said they could forget the hotdogs and beer, we wanted a share of the patronage."

Crawford said that after taking office he sought to establish a human rights council. The council was finally established, although in a much weaker form than Crawford wanted. Because of the watering down, Crawford said, "I voted against it in protest because I wanted something with teeth, but I wanted it to pass and I knew the votes were there. I wanted the record of history to show my objection. As it turned out, I had the worst 30 seconds of my career. After I voted 'No,' Dave Pottinger hesitated about 30 seconds and mumbled he wasn't sure. He finally voted for it."

Crawford said he is viewing the new crop of black leaders with considerable interest. He said he expects them to build on the ground that he, McLin, Mayor James H. McGee and other black politicians captured during the past decade.

"Back in the 1940s or 1950s, if you went to·100 people and asked them to name the three black leaders in town, nobody would have lifted an eyebrow. There were precious few of them. Now, if you ask, the first thing they would do is laugh. There's no one or two or five or 10 black leaders. Now, there's complete acceptance that no one presumes to speak for all blacks. I don't think there will ever be a time again when a couple of organizations can be thought of as the black organizations." Crawford added, about new black leaders, "I don't think you have to scream and curse white people, but you have to put yourself on the line against anyone who oppresses blacks and the poor."

During the interview, the reporter scribbled down several physical observations: Crawford is a fastidious dresser, with a penchant for brightly colored suits that are stylishly color-coordinated. He often changes suits in the middle of the day and keeps a spare suit in his office. He is a small man, about 5-feet-9, 140 pounds; lean and trim. He is aging gracefully as his hair is turning slowly to a dignified white. Now it is mostly black with a strong peppering of white. He has a neat moustache and keeps his hair trimmed short in the fashion popular with blacks before the Afro became style. He is a warm, friendly man, both publicly and privately, with many close friends among both blacks and whites. He is articulate, even in conversations.

As city commission clerk, the reporter noted that Crawford takes care of all administrative details for the elected officials, provides political advice, and serves as parliamentarian at commission meetings. He compiles the agenda for the commission meetings, thus exercising the power of determining, generally, what is to be discussed. He also participates in the city manager's staff meetings, often offering sage political advice.

From many city hall sources, the reporter has learned that Crawford's influence is heavy in all areas of city government. Other city hall powers like and respect Crawford, and regard him as a man of unquestionable integrity. White officials agree that Crawford has repeatedly shown concern not only for the black community, but for the city as a whole.

The reporter then talked to a young, up-and-coming black official who is a Crawford protege. The man said he had mixed feelings about Crawford's present role. "I don't think Don's influence is any less than when he was commissioner. Black people know what he's doing. He was smart enough to change his style when he switched into a staff position." He said that Crawford has an uncanny ability to communicate with anyone. "You can talk to militants or conservative blacks and they will tell you they respect him."

But, with a note of wishfulness, he added, "You should have heard that man speak when he was commissioner. He can be so eloquent, so effective. I know he's doing more than ever, but I guess I was a little disappointed when he stepped down."

Later, the reporter visited State Representative C.J. McLin Jr. at his West Dayton mortuary, which he inherited from his late father. McLin, a powerful political force in the black community and in the Ohio Legislature, was guarded in selecting comments to make about Crawford. As a close personal friend, McLin seemed concerned about unintentionally saying anything that might damage Crawford's position.

McLin chucked and nodded to affirm Crawford's anecdote about his demand for patronage instead of hotdogs and beer. The reporter asked for anecdotes about Crawford and McLin lapsed into silent thought, punctuated by an occasional mischievous chuckle. "No, I can't tell you that one," he said repeatedly, without elaboration.

McLin explained that when Crawford sought re-election, he had a good chance of winning the most votes of any candidate. This would have meant that he would have served as the city's first black mayor. "A team of reporters from a national magazine followed Don around. Among them was an attractive blonde from Sweden. We were walking into an East Side (a predominantly white, conservative area) speaking engagement and she was walking beside him. I grabbed her arm and said, "You can't walk in with him, I'll explain later."

Dave Hall narrowly won more votes to become mayor, but Crawford, who finished second in the voting, retained his commission seat.

McLin said that after the election, he and Crawford were on the opposite sides of an issue which would discard the city management form of government and return to a strong mayor government. McLin and the Democratic party, which controlled city politics, saw that they could obtain many more patronage positions through the strong mayor system, but Crawford, a Democrat also, decided that the city would suffer under such a system, so he headed a campaign to retain the city manager system.

In the campaign, McLin recalled, "I invited Crawford over to the Democratic club. When he came, I got him to debate me. I knew I had him on my grounds. Crawford knew he had been had and right in the middle of the debate he whispered, 'You dirty so-and-so.'"

The reporter again contacted Crawford, who laughed when he heard McLin's account. Crawford said that many right-wing organizations joined the campaign on the side of the strong-mayor form of government, and flooded the city with mud-slinging, racist campaign material. "That was the bitterest, nastiest treatment I ever ran into in politics. Most practical politicians said I had to be crazy to take on an issue where I could lose everything and gain nothing."

The reporter then contacted Joe Wine, a city bureaucrat who had served on the commission with Crawford. He said, "Through patience and good will, he would convince the others. Don would win in the long run and get support.

Being the kind of guy he was as the first black was so important. That made all the difference." Wine added that Crawford greatly improved communications with citizens. "Don believed strongly in the importance of having citizens understand what was happening. He used to insist on stopping and talking about issues that were being approved mechanically. Often, Don and I would pretend to get into an argument to get other commissioners talking."

The reporter talked to many other friends, colleagues and enemies of Crawford, but decided that the information contained in the interviews, above, was sufficient and representative. Other material simply substantiated or elaborated on the nature of the human being named Don Crawford, as was depicted in these interviews.

Using the editing and rewriting techniques discussed in earlier chapters, the reporter spent several hours shaping the story in his mind and looking for the proper approach in relating it. Realizing that, because of the limitations of newspaper format, he could not capture the whole, complex man, the reporter attempted to capture the *essence* of the man.

The reporter quickly recognized still another limitation: a white reporter cannot reasonably hope to fully understand—much less communicate—the special viewpoint and experiences of being black. The cultural differences between the reporter and the story subject are far too great to bridge in even a lengthy series of interviews. Instead, the reporter carefully allowed the subject, his friends, colleagues and adversaries to provide that insight through quotations.

Another common research problem was evident in the interview with McLin. Friends of the story subject often withhold priceless anecdotes if there is even the faintest possibility that the anecdotes would cause an unfavorable reaction to the subject. Rarely does a reporter find a friend who is willing to shed light on the subject's "warts" as well as his virtues.

When the reporter entered the serious writing stage, his first obstacle was to decide on a lead. Normally, the reporter will resort to one of these lead types for a personal profile story:

1. *A Narrative Lead,* which entails a fast, exciting start by placing the subject in the midst of action.

2. *A Quotation Lead,* which lets the subject give considerable insight to his own character through a profound quotation.

3. *A Descriptive Lead,* which quickly establishes a strong mental image of the subject in the minds of readers to give them the psychological identification factor.

4. *A Combination Lead,* often that of a quotation and description, that uses the best elements of two or more leads to gain that vital initial impact.

As was discussed in Chapter 3, an overriding factor in choosing a lead is the exact nature of the material available. In the Crawford story, the quotations are generally good, but not profound enough for a quotation lead. No really dramatic action is available for a narrative lead.

So, the reporter quickly turns to his favorite type of lead: a descriptive lead. He combines it with a hint of a summary lead. Here is how the story begins:

> A frosting of white has crept into Don L. Crawford's hair since he became the first black to win a Dayton City Commission seat 12 years ago.
>
> The cheers of blacks hailing a city hall champion have subsided since he quit the commission in 1967, eventually becoming executive assistant to the city commission.
>
> Television camera lights focus on him only rarely now and reporters no longer eagerly place quotation marks around his most casual comments.

It could be argued, with justification, that the lead actually continues for three paragraphs. After creating the initial physical image, the reporter lingers for several paragraphs to set up the body of the story. As you will note as the story unfolds, the body of a personal profile story is even more amorphous than other features. The reporter allows reader interest to solely determine story organization, so, as long as the story remains concise and interesting, he makes no attempt to fit it into any standard structure.

The story continues:

> To some, Crawford may appear to be the kind of lingering political ghost that haunts a city hall bureaucracy long after his productive days are behind him.
>
> But political observers consider Don Crawford to be even more powerful and effective now than he ever was as a city commissioner.
>
> People who govern the city listen respectfully to the words of Don Crawford. City commissioners, department heads, and politicians at various levels of government view him as a sort of black guru of politics.
>
> His casual, relaxed appearance is deceiving.
>
> "Don is the sort of guy where, if you dumped a bucket of water on him while he slept, he would wake up and say just the right thing for the situation," said State Rep. C. J. McLin, D-Dayton, his close friend.

"When I quit the commission, many people were disappointed in me," Crawford said. "They felt they were losing their champion in city hall. I was a symbolic creature.

"It wasn't easy for the casual observer to see that more often than not the vote was 4-1 or 3-2 against me. Crawford was a hero, but things weren't getting done."

"Now it's different, without the fanfare, commissioners pay more attention to me," he said. "The people probably have an advocate in a stronger position to help."

His influence on commissioners, he said, is above-board. "You do it simply by doing the job they hired you to do. They ask for my opinion and I give it to them."

A young black city official, a Crawford protege, admitted he has mixed feelings about Crawford's present role.

"I don't think Don's influence is any less than when he was commissioner," he said. "Black people know what he's doing. He was smart enough to change his style when he switched to a staff position."

The man, who asked not to be identified, said Crawford has an uncanny ability to communicate. "You can talk to militants or conservative blacks and they will tell you they respect him."

But almost wishfully, he added, "You should have heard that man speak when he was commissioner. He can be so eloquent, so effective.

"I know he's doing more than ever, but I guess I was a little disappointed when he stepped down."

No one in city hall disputes that Don Crawford is a powerful political force.

But his rise to power is almost as intriguing as the power itself.

"I stumbled into Dayton, fell into Boy Scout work, and got pushed into the commission," Crawford said.

Crawford, born July 27, 1921, in Clinton, Ky., is the son of a railroad chef. "We moved around a lot," he recalled.

At Kentucky State College, he said, "I started into medicine but my ego sidetracked me. Ever since I was a kid, I wanted to be one of the very best in whatever I did.

"I found out it would take a lot of money and probably some study in Europe to be one of the very best in medicine."

So Crawford settled for a career in scientific research, picking up a bachelor of science degree in mathematics and physics.

After graduating in 1942, he taught high school classes for a year, hoping to get an Army Air Corps commission during the war. When that failed to materialize, he enlisted in the Navy becoming one of the first black quartermasters.

When the war ended, he married his college sweetheart, Agatha, who was teaching in Dayton.

"I came to pick her up here in April 1946," he said. "We thought we were going to Chicago to start life there, but I had to wait a few months for her to finish the term and I stumbled into scouting."

Crawford took a job as a district scout executive. By 1951, he was the assistant executive for the Miami Valley Scout Region.

"What really sold me on scouting and Dayton was I found I could walk into the vice president's office at a place like NCR (National Cash Register) and get his time and attention because I was there on scouting.

"If Dayton was that kind of community with that kind of leadership, it deserved some looking into," Crawford said.

By 1961, the All-Dayton Committee (a powerful political organization) and black leaders decided time was ripe for a black city commissioner. They needed a black candidate with some appeal to white voters.

"People at least knew Don Crawford and knew me as a Boy Scout leader, and that's a clean, healthy image to carry," he said.

Crawford claimed he had no political affiliations or ambitions prior to that race, although C. J. McLin Sr., a powerful black politician, and his son, "Mac Junior," were among his friends.

"Mac Senior had run for commission before, and he was terribly mistreated, even threatened," Crawford said. "But he was always sure that a black could be elected.

"Long before I ever thought about running, he (Mac Senior) said, 'Someday, son, I predict you will be the first black city commissioner'."

A decided underdog, Crawford said he ran into little mudslinging. "People were very decent to me all over town," he said, adding, "They thought I had no chance.

"As late as 9 O'clock election night, some people pretended to be friendly who were pleased to see me running fourth. The West Dayton votes came in later, however, and I jumped to a strong second. I received a fair vote in the rest of the city."

Crawford's election caused jubilation in West Dayton. "There was quite a celebration," he said. "Mac Senior literally cried because he was so overjoyed that his prediction was true."

With Crawford and C. J. McLin Jr. leading the new black political surge, the nature of Dayton politics changed.

"For years, the (Democratic) party would set up free hotdogs and beer on the West Side every election," Crawford recalled. "Mac Junior finally said they could forget the hotdogs and beer, we wanted a share of the patronage."

McLin chuckled and nodded in affirmation when told of Crawford's anecdote. In Crawford's second campaign, it appeared he might get the most votes and become mayor.

"A team of reporters from a national magazine followed Don

around," McLin recalled. "Among them was an attractive blonde from Sweden.

"We were walking in to an East Side speaking engagement and she was walking beside him. I grabbed her arm and said, 'You can't walk in with him, I'll explain later.' "

Dave Hall edged out Crawford for the mayor's gavel, but Crawford did retain his commission seat.

After winning re-election, Crawford and McLin found themselves on opposite sides over a movement to scrap the city manager form of government in favor of a strong mayor system.

McLin and local Democrats saw a harvest of patronage plums in the strong-mayor system, but Crawford decided the city would suffer, so he led the campaign to save the city management system.

Crawford said right wing groups jumped in on the strong mayor side of the fence and flooded the city with mud-slinging, racist material.

"That was the bitterest, nastiest treatment I ever ran into in politics," Crawford said. "Most practical politicians said I had to be crazy to take on an issue where I could lose everything and gain nothing."

McLin recalled the campaign with a chuckle. "I invited Crawford over to the Democratic club," he said. "When he came, I got him to debate me. I knew I had him on my grounds.

"Crawford knew he had been had and right in the middle of the debate he whispered, 'You dirty so-and-so.' "

Meanwhile, Crawford blossomed into a powerful commissioner. Joe Wine, who served on the commission with Crawford, said, "Through patience and good will, he would convince the others. Don would win in the long-run and get support.

"Being the kind of guy he was as the first black was so important. That made all the difference."

Wine said that Crawford greatly improved communications with citizens.

"Don believed strongly in the importance of having citizens understand what was happening," Wine said.

"He used to insist on stopping and talking about issues that were being approved mechanically. Often, Don and I would pretend to get into an argument to get other commissioners talking," Wine added.

Crawford said he is particularly proud of his fight to establish a human rights council, although the version that was passed under his tenure was, he said, much weaker than he wanted. The vote to create the council gave him a scare.

"I voted against it in protest because I wanted something with teeth, but I wanted it to pass and I knew the votes were there," he said. "I wanted the record of history to show my objection.

"As it turned out, I had the worst 30 seconds of my career.

After I voted 'No,' Dave Pottinger hesitated about 30 seconds and mumbled he wasn't sure. He finally voted for it."

With considerable interest, he sees a new crop of black leaders emerging to hold and expand the ground that he, McLin, Mayor James H. McGee and other black politicians captured during the past decade.

"Back in the 1940s or 1950s, if you went to 100 people and asked them to name the three black leaders in town, nobody would have lifted an eyebrow. There were precious few of them.

"Now, if you ask, the first thing they would do is laugh. There's no one or two or five or 10 black leaders.

"Now, there's complete acceptance that no one presumes to speak for all blacks. I don't think there will ever be a time again when a couple of organizations can be thought of as the black organizations."

As for the new black leaders, he said, "I don't think you have to scream and curse white people, but you have to put yourself on the line against anyone who oppresses blacks and the poor."

TRICKS OF WRITING PROFILES

In analyzing the story, you will note that each segment of material is worked into the story so smoothly that the reader is hardly aware that the source of the material has changed. When the McLin interview was inserted, the State Representative entered by nodding his head and chuckling at a Crawford anecdote, which was told to the reporter two days previously. The effect is as though McLin and Crawford are sitting in the same room.

The writer should never be blunt and clumsy, when introducing new segments of material, by leading in with such a phrase as, "In a later interview, McLin confirmed the Crawford anecdote . . ."

A second trick of writing profiles is to use anecdotes liberally. Anecdotes, you will recall, are used as gems to salt the mine of the story. In a personal profile, anecdotes also serve to add great depth to the character you are capturing.

Crawford's recollection of his worst 30 seconds, when it appeared his human rights council would be killed by his protest vote, was both amusing and informative about the man who was so concerned with the historical record of his action.

SUMMARY

After spending several days or weeks working on such a story, it is natural for a reporter to look back at the effort and the resulting story and ask the question: Was it worth the effort? Or, did I succeed in telling the story?

Success in writing profiles is often difficult to determine. If the story subject compliments the reporter after the story is printed, then he may have succeeded only in writing a publicity release. If the subject is angry, then the reporter may have made a serious error, or he may have simply been painfully honest.

Rarely can a feature writer ascertain the effectiveness of a personal profile. Reader feedback is normally very light.

Perhaps the best means of determining the value and validity of the story is to read the story slowly from the viewpoint of the reader. If, in your judgment, the reader gains valuable insight and understanding of the subject, then the story was a success.

EXERCISES

Exercise 1.

Using the information from which the story was written, write your own version of the Don Crawford profile, using a different lead and a different story organization.

Exercise 2.

Write a narrative lead, a quotation lead, a descriptive lead and a combination lead, using the material given in the research section.

Exercise 3.

Write a personal profile story about your roommate, a professor, a relative, or someone else whom you know quite well.

13 : Seasonal Stories

The calendar plays an important role in dictating the nature of feature coverage. The public is accustomed to centering its activities through the year around several special holidays, holiday seasons and annual events. The newspaper feature writer is often expected to supply stories to help create the proper mood for a given annual event.

Religious holidays, particularly Christian holidays, are especially dominating to feature coverage. Many larger newspapers will assign such feature coverage to one or two general assignments reporters during the long holiday stretch from Thanksgiving through Christmas.

Other journalists will draw special feature assignments for Easter, Independence Day, Presidents' Day, Halloween and St. Valentine's Day.

Regardless of which holiday a reporter covers, he will encounter one major obstacle: conceiving an angle for a story that hasn't been done hundreds of times before.

By definition, a seasonal feature story is an account of an annual event or an aspect of that annual event which captures its spirit.

The seasonal feature may fall into almost any of the feature categories discussed in previous chapters. It may be a color story on an Independence Day fireworks festival, or a human interest feature about a family that has no money or shelter at Christmas.

A major difference between a seasonal feature and other features is that the tone and theme of the seasonal feature is firmly established by the season.

Christmas features, for example, may deal specifically with religious aspects, the Santa Claus theme, or the general spirit of human joy and kindness which is associated with the holiday. While these areas are broad, a Christmas seasonal feature must tie into one of those overall themes.

FINDING THE ANGLE

As was mentioned earlier, the greatest obstacle for the journalist is finding that elusive, different angle. In coping with that problem, many reporters use these three approaches:

1. Use your imagination and well-trained power of observation to see the unusual or interesting things which escape the attention of other people.

2. Always be alert for someone who has a unique or different viewpoint from which to observe the event.

3. Assume that although some reporter somewhere and at some time may have done the same feature or a variation of it, it was not done in your city, or not for a long time.

The first approach often requires hours of walking or driving around the city with an eye cocked for small details. After several hours, the reporter may see an amputee selling pencils from a wheelchair parked on a busy downtown sidewalk. It's Christmas season and shoppers are everywhere.

The reporter may stop to chat with the man. The angle is obvious: With the spirit-of-giving theme, do people give more to the needy? Regardless of the answer, the reporter has his feature story.

Perhaps an outdoor skating rink has been erected in a downtown plaza by merchants who want to provide entertainment for children while parents shop. Among the children, an elderly woman neatly performs a perfect figure-8. Even the most unimaginative reporter could see a feature story about the skating grandmother amid the happy children.

The second approach is similar. The reporter simply looks for someone who may see an unusual aspect of the same event that thousands of other people see.

Perhaps, at the Independence Day celebration in Greeley, Colorado, an elderly man is attending his 50th Independence Day Stampede rodeo. He has seen all of the great rodeo cowboys over a half century, so he can provide a special viewpoint from which to watch the young crop of modern bronco-busters.

The viewpoint of children is such a consistent story-producer that one would think that it would bore readers after so much use. Yet, adults are invariably fascinated by the special world of a 7-year-old child.

A routine story assignment for the lighting of the downtown Christmas decorations can become a beautiful feature as seen through the eyes of a 5-year-old, who describes what *she* sees to the reporter.

The last approach is perhaps the most frequently used. A reporter may contend, with justification, that all of the really interesting feature ideas have been done by the generations of journalists who annually search for them.

How many reporters have donned Santa Claus costumes? How many stories have been written about Living Nativity Scenes? How many feature writers have followed small children on Easter Egg hunts? How many feature stories, from every conceivable angle, have been done on Halloween Trick-or-Treating?

The questions are irrelevant. Instead, the astute reporter will ask: Has any reporter ever played Santa Claus in *this city*? If so, has the story been done in recent years?

If the answers to the latter questions are negative, then the reporter may feel free to research and write the story, even though he knows it has been done somewhere, sometime before. The reporter is interested in finding a new story that *his* readers haven't seen.

It should be noted that borrowing story ideas from other out-of-town newspapers is a cherished journalistic tradition. A newsstand which sells out-of-town newspapers often becomes a favorite hangout for reporters and editors. A scandal in Colorado may inspire investigation in Ohio, and a cute feature idea in Kansas may be borrowed to entertain readers in Nevada.

FOLLOWING THE SEASONAL FEATURE CALENDAR

Hardly a month passes without at least one seasonal feature event which, by tradition and, perhaps, because of reader expectation, demands coverage. Let's examine the feature calendar and consider some feature angles for each.

New Year's Day

Newspapers frequently begin the new year with traditional feature coverage. Newspapers in cities which host football bowls devote pages to features about the big event that brings so much money and prestige to their cities.

In New Orleans, a reporter may cover the traditional post-game celebrations along famous Bourbon Street where fans from the two participating schools gather in packed night spots to hurl school yells at each other and greet the new year after the New Year's Eve game.

Looking for that different angle, he may follow a cheerleader from the winning school, or a band member from the losing school.

Many cities have New Year's Day parades, particularly Pasadena, Calif. and Dallas, Tex., which also host football games. The viewpoint of a small child at a parade is always fascinating.

Away from the happy crowds, reporters in other cities may pursue the age-old New Year's Day resolutions story by asking passers by whether they made any resolutions.

Perhaps another reporter may seek out "football widows" whose husbands sit, entranced, in front of the television sets to watch 10 hours of consecutive football.

St. Valentine's Day

Visits to various greeting card shops can produce a feature about human nature. What kinds of cards are most popular this year? Are people buying less expensive cards because of tight economic conditions? Do people have unusual requests for cards?

Candy stores, gift shops and other stores that normally profit by St. Valentine's Day can produce similar viewpoints.

Local schools provide still another angle. Do children exchange Valentines in class? A reporter may attend such a session and note the strange candor of children. Which child received the most cards? Why does he or she think this happened? Are any children embarrassed? Or heartbroken over the lack of a card?

Presidents' Day

Again, children may provide the best angle for this day which honors Presidents Washington and Lincoln. The humorous conceptions —and misconceptions—of children about the identities and accomplishments of the Presidents can be hilarious.

Bookstores may produce another angle: has there been an increased demand for books about the Presidents?

Easter—Passover

Except for the Easter Egg hunt tradition, the atmosphere surrounding these great religious events is somewhat somber and dignified, despite the great joy of deliverence that is an overriding theme.

Churches and synagogues are literally filled with appropriate feature stories.

A reporter may survey several Christian ministers about their views of that strange annual church creature called an "Easter Bunny": a member who attends church only at Easter.

The faith of the elderly is always a good feature possibility, particularly at Easter. The special viewpoints of an octogenarian couple who steady each other in their feeble but determined walk to an altar rail can be a touching and meaningful picture of faith.

An interview with Jewish rabbis and members of the Jewish community about the meaning, impact and tradition of Passover may not only produce a meaningful feature story, but it could increase understanding between the Jewish and Christian communities.

The Easter Egg tradition is an opportunity for a lighter approach. Parents everywhere find delight by watching young children plunge into bushes in search of the brightly colored eggs. A reporter may be pressed to find that different angle to this well-worn story, yet, with imagination, a different twist is usually available.

A child who recently recovered her sight after a delicate operation may see wonders that no one has seen before. A reporter may share her discoveries with thousands of readers through a feature story on her first *look* at an Easter Egg hunt.

Memorial Day

A traditional start to the vacation season, Memorial Day is one of several holidays that seem to have lost its meaning amid celebration. While people may vaguely be aware of wreath-layings at Arlington National Cemetery, many are much too busy enjoying outings to dwell on such serious thoughts.

A good feature writer may not let readers forget. Interviews with proud old veterans of World War I or young, serious men who fought in Vietnam may remind readers of the purpose of the day.

Fourth of July

While the event may receive superficial observance in most large cities, the Fourth of July is often a major event of the year in smaller cities and towns.

A feature writer naturally gravitates to where the festive crowds gather.

For instance, the Greeley, Colorado Independence Day Stampede is, to the local citizenry, what the Rose Bowl is to the people of Pasadena, California.

Months before July 4th, committees are formed and plans are made. Four days before Independence Day, a rodeo begins, featuring top cowboys and cowgirls from all over the West.

Free Bar-B-Cues are sponsored by local merchants to which everyone is invited. Thousands of people happily stand in line, chatting with strangers, while waiting on the food.

Fireworks extravaganza, a parade filled with horses, and a multitude of American flags everywhere provide the entertainment and atmosphere.

Any journalist who attended could find a score of excellent feature story ideas.

Other communities stage celebrations that are in keeping with their own traditions. Certainly, no reporter should have to travel more than 10 miles from his city to find an Independence Day celebration.

Labor Day

As Memorial Day serves as the beginning of the summer vacation season, Labor Day serves as the end. A trip to almost any outdoor recreational facility will produce a thick crowd of people working on a last fling before public schools reopen.

A besieged life-guard at a public swimming pool may provide a feature angle, as he desperately tries to keep order and safety in the mob of revelers.

Beaches and resorts are also prime sources of Labor Day features, possibly from the viewpoint of a hotel manager.

A more serious viewpoint may be obtained by riding with a state highway patrolman, who has the unpleasant task of dealing with throngs of intoxicated motorists and providing emergency assistance to automobile accident victims.

Halloween

The gruesome costumes, mischievous tricks, and the interaction between the children and adults can provide ample feature topics.

A reporter may complete his research in his own home by observing the behavior of the children. Some children are afraid of the adults and are literally dragged before the door by older brothers and sisters. Others seem to fear nothing, even demanding more candy than the stingy offering of a single stick of chewing gum.

The tricks that befall the reporter's property can at least provide story fodder. The soaped windows, the smashed pumpkin on the driveway, and even the firecracker in the mailbox may give the readers a chuckle.

A walk with young children may prove productive. The reporter may gather observations on how adults react to the small monsters.

The aftermath may provide interviews with victims of bizarre tricks. A Volkswagen owner may find that pranksters carried his car into his fenced yard. Misplaced outhouses, padlocked tool sheds, and stuffed mailboxes are standard pranks.

Thanksgiving

A visit to a farm that sells hundreds of pumpkins to passing motorists can provide interesting insight to human nature. How do people select a pumpkin? What can you do with the insides of a pumpkin when you make a jack-o-lantern? What does the farmer do with unsold pumpkins?

School Thanksgiving programs may also provide stories as 8-year-old Miles Standishs blurt out traditional lines or suffer from stage fright.

As noted in earlier chapters, an imaginative reporter produce his own Thanksgiving story, such as the Great Turkey Hunt.

Christmas

Feature stories are so abundant at Christmas that the reporter may find himself faced with the job of deciding which to write and which to discard.

A walk through the downtown area may produce a dozen fine feature ideas.

Several children are gathered around a display window at a major downtown department store, watching the animated elves and angels. The reporter may simply interview the children for reaction, then go inside to interview the person who set up or designed the display.

While inside, he may wander to the toy department and chat with clerks about the most popular toys of the year and, perhaps, changing trends in toy purchases. Or, he may talk to shoppers to see whether they are concerned about the safety of toys.

A Salvation Army worker, ringing a bell before a collection pot, may provide interesting observations about people at Christmas.

A traffic policeman, directing the swarm of cars, may provide insight to the darker side of human nature at Christmas.

Walking a few blocks from the central business district, the reporter may talk to the people on "skid row" who may have no Christmas.

The only limit to the number of features a reporter can produce during Christmas season is his time and energy.

Seasonal Events

Not all seasonal features concern holidays. Each part of the country has its own, peculiar celebrations, festivities or special annual event.

Although you won't find it marked in red on your calendar, the return of the buzzards on March 15th is a yearly highlight to the residents of Hinckley, Ohio. On the same day, year after year, the normally unpopular scavengers flock to the small Ohio town. No one can establish scientifically just why the buzzards come. Local townspeople don't particularly care. The point is that the buzzards always return, and the town celebrates. Few reporters could miss this feature angle.

Half a continent away, the first cool days of October provide a different excitement for Coloradans who flock to the mountains to watch the green aspen trees turn to a brilliant yellow. Roads are packed with tourists who take rolls of films along to capture the beauty.

Gulf Coast residents flock to New Orleans for the jubilent Mardi Gras celebration. Southerners pour onto backroads when the dogwood trees bloom in the spring. All across the nation, special events abound to keep feature writers well occupied.

Various firsts of new seasons are also of interest to readers. The first appreciable snowfall, the first day of Spring, the longest and shortest days of the year are events worth noting through feature coverage.

It should be stressed that the traditional nature of these basic story sources should, in no way, stifle a reporter's creativity. Just as New Year's Eve provides an occasion for a party, a seasonal event provides the occasion for a feature story. In either case, the nature of the party-story is, in no way, dictated by the event. Instead, the nature is dependent on the outlook and creativity of the human mind.

Writing a Seasonal Story

Because of the wide range of applicability among the various types of features, no particular set of writing guidelines can be established for seasonal features.

Instead, the writer should simply keep a single rule in mind: avoid seasonal clichés.

Such over-worked, traditional terms as "Merry Christmas," "Happy New Year," "Mr. Longears" (Easter Bunny), "Jolly Old Saint Nick," "Turkey Day," or "Be My Valentine," have become unimaginative clichés.

While they are fine for greeting cards, they tend to detract from feature stories, particularly when used repeatedly.

A good writer can communicate the basic messages inherent in such clichés, without actually saying them. Instead of saying, "Merry Christmas," the writer depicts a joyous Christmas family scene to more effectively convey that meaning.

Summary

Much of the success of writing quality seasonal features depends on the reporter's ability to view the world around him with excitement and fascination. The more serious side of journalism tends to create cynics with jaded outlooks. Yet, given the opportunity to write seasonal features, the creative writer that lurks beneath the reporter's jaded exterior is released to bask in the warmth of special seasonal events, viewing them with the excited outlook of a child.

EXERCISES

1. Write a list of 10 seasonal feature story ideas for the Christmas season. For each idea, explain how you would collect the material needed for your story.

2. Depending on the current season, write a seasonal feature story about the first snow, Thanksgiving, Christmas season, Presidents' Day, St. Valentine's Day, the first day of Spring, Memorial Day, or Independence Day. If there is a local celebration of another event, you may write about it.

14 Aftermath Stories

Late at night, the telephone rings insistently until a bleary-eyed reporter finally gropes for the receiver and mumbles a greeting.

After listening for a moment, he grunts a note of affirmation, briefly explains the situation to his wife, then dresses and dashes to his car for a fast ride to the State University campus.

The caller was the city editor, who informed the reporter that a riot at the campus had spilled over into the shops off campus, causing a great deal of damage. It was 11:15 p.m. The city editor wanted an early edition story by 8 a.m.

The city editor didn't have to explain what type of story he expected from the reporter. The situation obviously called for an aftermath feature story.

By definition, an aftermath story is a featurized follow-up to a disaster, tragedy or profound news event that captures the impact and dimensions of the event by humanizing its effect.

The university is 60 miles from the reporter's city and the event, the rioting, had started hours earlier. Unless the rioting was of major insurrection proportions, local authorities would have it contained by the time the reporter arrived. In any case, the Associated Press and United Press International would be flooding their teletype wires with information about the disorders before the reporter even left his own city.

Even if the reporter should reach the scene in time to cover the confrontations, he would be limited in acquiring information by the fact that he isn't familiar with local law enforcement officials, nor with student activists. Reporters from the university's host city would keep well ahead of out-of-town journalists through their advantage of knowing sources on each side of the confrontation. And these reporters are obliged to feed their information to the wire services and, indirectly, to the reporter's own newspaper.

With all of these disadvantages, the newspaper is still willing to undertake the expense of sending a reporter to cover the event for two reasons:

1. *Prestige.* If the event is significant enough, staff coverage is a point of honor, of pride. By sending a staff reporter, the newspaper is telling readers that "our guys" are top professionals who can—and do—cover everything.

2. *The Local Angle.* Somewhere in the chaos of confrontation or controversy, someone from the reporter's city may be involved. Perhaps a hometown student witnessed a clash between activist students and campus policemen. Perhaps another hometown student was injured by a rock, or by a teargas cannister.

Regardless, many university alumni live in the reporter's town, and others have relatives and friends in the university town. The effect of a riot at a state institution has many indirect affects on each person in the state, such as higher taxes and a weaker educational institution, at least in the aftermath period.

Quickly ruling out hard news coverage, the reporter decides to write an aftermath feature which may run as a sidebar to the wire service accounts which pool information from every available news source.

While the wire service busily tells readers what happened, the local reporter will show readers the effect in human terms.

Aftermath stories may take one of several approaches:

1. *The epitomy of the victim or the victims.* The reporter may find a survivor of a mass tragedy, such as a flood, tornado or fire, and intensively interview that survivor and use his story as a vehicle to stress the overall human aspects of the event. If none of the main characters survived, or are inaccessible, then the reporter may talk to friends and relatives to recreate the character in print and explain how this human being came to be in the fateful place at the fateful time.

2. *The mood piece.* Concentrate on describing the scene and the people at the scene after the event, emphasizing ironies and the different perspectives of the survivors.

3. *The hero.* If there's hero material available, gather it and, if possible, interview the hero. Note that at the scene of such heroism, by-standers often chat excitedly about a brave deed. An alert reporter should quickly pick up such rumor.

4. *The goat.* If someone accidentally caused the tragedy, the potential for a truly dramatic account is even greater than in hero angles. Such stories are difficult to find, because the "goat" of a tragedy is, normally, understandably reluctant to accept the public spotlight for his blunder.

The nature of the event often dictates the approach a reporter should use.

With the example of a campus riot, the mood piece is probably the most applicable. Heros and goats can too easily become propaganda tools in such controversies. If a student is a hero or a goat, then there is a strong, underlying implication that students involved in the incident were either right or wrong in their contention. A journalist may not draw such judgemental conclusions. The same is true with victims. If the student is a "victim," then a law enforcement person is the aggressor. This may or may not be true. In most cases, such conclusions, either way, would be inaccurate or, at the very least, simplistic renditions of events.

Fire stories are often producers of heros or goats.

When covering the aftermath of a fatal fire in which two children were killed, the police reporter may overhear neighbors talking about a teenage boy who rescued three younger children by carrying them out of a second story attic window, down the sloping roof, then dropping them to the ground from a low overhang.

A goat may have been a cigarette smoker who fell asleep while smoking in bed, causing the fire. Or, perhaps, another youth was cleaning automobile parts with gasoline, unaware that gasoline fumes, which are heavier than air, float downward and drift across floors. When gasoline fumes find a space heater or a floor furnace, an explosion and fire result.

After a tornado (see chapter 11), the victims, or the epitomy of victims is perhaps most appropriate as people read the verbatim accounts and comments of survivors, easily identifying with them.

WRITING THE AFTERMATH STORY

In writing an aftermath story, the need to arouse human empathy overrides other considerations. The writer must stir the reader's imagination because, otherwise, the reader can simply obtain the facts without undue elaboration in the main news story.

1. *Play heavily on human emotion.*

Sorrow, fear, happiness, vanity and other vital human emotions will captivate the reader, once they are stirred. If, for example, a reader's fear is aroused, he must continue to read the article until it is resolved.

2. *Try to make the reader identify with the victims.*

Perhaps the best of all feature stories are the ones that elicit the feeling of, "There, but for the grace of God, go I" from the reader. Psychologists say that identification is a very strong human impulse which often comes in the form of hero-worshiping. Any child who has collected sports-hero cards, or read adventure books and magazines indulged in a vicarious adventure through identification. When Ken Stabler completes a touchdown pass, or Billie Jean King wins a tennis match, thousands of sports partisans feel that, for a brief moment, *they* were the sports heros.

To a lesser degree, the reader may enjoy a similar thrill by reading about a 14-year-old boy who rescues his younger brothers from a fire; or a 15-year-old girl who captures a burglar by swatting him with a baseball bat.

3. *Write very tersely and briefly.*

As discussed in the chapter on sidebar features, the need for brevity is great when the success of the story may greatly depend on its placement. The success of an aftermath story may well depend on whether it can "ride the coattails" of the main story by running on the same page as a sidebar.

4. *Concentrate on a fast-moving, strong lead.*

Normally, the writer may seek a descriptive lead or a narrative lead to find the strong lead approach necessary to capture the reader's attention immediately.

The need to create a mental image, immediately, is very strong. The reader must be able to "see" the subject, if he is to strongly identify with that subject.

The reporter who arrived to cover the campus riot may easily find the necessary elements for a good aftermath feature story, but he may still face many tough, sometimes hazardous, hours of work collecting that material.

Arriving at the university, the reporter parks off campus, several blocks from the area in which most of the violence had occurred. He knows the great value of transportation, so he decides to protect the car.

As he walks to the main area of troubled activity, he stops to chat with students.

Reporter: "What's going on?"

Student A: "Beats me. I heard about a riot on the radio, but I haven't seen a thing. I guess we're having one, but, frankly, I couldn't care less."

Student B: "Yeah, we've seen lots of cops driving by, but no one has fought with them that I've seen. Maybe it's going down across campus, that's what the radio said."

Reporter: "Do you know why the riot broke out?"

Student B: "Not really. There have been lots of little incidents, such as picketing, against the ROTC program. But no one really expected anything like this to happen."

Student A: "I couldn't care less about who's right or wrong. All I want is my degree. I've worked awfully hard for four years to get that thing, so I don't want to see the school closed so I have to come back another quarter."

Walking to the main street that connected campus with downtown, the reporter sees a concentration of Sheriff's deputies who are waiting impatiently for orders to move to a troubled area. The deputies are wearing riot helmets, gas masks, and carrying shotguns and long nightsticks. Police car windows are taped to prevent shattering should a rock strike.

Deputy: "Who are you and what are you doing here?"

Reporter: (Identifying himself). "Who's in charge?"

Deputy: (suspiciously) "Talk to Lt. Samuels of the city police, he's in charge."

Lt. Samuels is much easier to deal with than the understandably nervous deputy.

Samuels: "We've pretty well got everything under control now, except for a few roving bands. They hit Monument Street about 9:30 p.m., about 80 students, and they knocked out every store window for a seven-block area. We broke their charge at about 9:50 with a wedge of about 45 officers. There were several minor injuries, but no one was seriously hurt."

Reporter: "Any arrests?"

Samuels: "We have about a dozen on various charges relating to the confrontation. Another half dozen or so are being patched up at the hospital."

A helicopter flew over, shining a powerful search light that dangled a cable beneath it.

Reporter: "What's that for?"

Samuels: "It's a precaution against snipers. If any of our units catch sniper fire from roof tops, the chopper will suppress the fire. Our best sharpshooter is riding in the chopper."

Moving into the damaged area, the reporter talks to merchants who are unhappily cleaning up debris.

Reporter: "Why did they do it?"

Merchant: "I can't tell you why, I don't know. It's nothing personal, I don't think. I've always got along well with the students, I like them and I try to be fair to them. They were just on a rampage, it's disgusting.

"Before you go print that, keep one other thing in mind: Only about 70 or 80 of them did this. About 12,000 of them had nothing at all to do with this."

Walking along Monument Street, assessing the damage, the reporter encounters a patrol car filled with half a dozen grim police officers.

Police Sergeant: "May I see your identification, sir?"

Reporter: (Showing press card) "It seems pretty quiet, now. Is everything under control?"

Sergeant: "Pretty well, except for roving bands who are going around, beating up anyone who looks like a plainclothes policeman. And you look a whole lot like a plainclothesman."

Suddenly, the reporter hears the roar of powerful truck engines. Looking up, he sees dozens of trucks carrying National Guardsmen speed down Monument Street. The soldiers quickly jump from the trucks and position themselves to seal off the campus.

Reporter: "I'll bet you were upset when you found out that you had been called up."

Soldier: "You had better believe it. Any way you look at it, we get the short end of the stick. The students are mad at us and call us names. The cops are grumpy as the devil about us taking over. The reporters always give us bad coverage. Yeah, I'm not too happy about being here."

The reporter then walks along sidestreets where many students have apartments, to chat with students who sit on front steps to discuss the excitement.

Reporter: "Just how did it get started?"

Student: "I didn't see it myself, but I heard that some demonstrators started pitching rocks at the campus police after they ordered the demonstrators to disperse."

Second Student: "I heard another version. I heard that a girl was carrying a sign and a cop came up to her and beat her over the head for no reason. Then a lot of her friends jumped him. He called for help and it built into this."

Third Student: "I don't know what happened, but I did see one cop try to give first aid to a girl who had been hit by a rock. When he bent over to help her, a guy got him in the side with a brick. It must have broken some ribs."

Forth student: "Yeah, maybe so. But the cop's friends threw a tear gas cannister into my math class. Yeah, we were just sitting there in class when the cop pitched it through the open window. It almost wiped us out before we could get out."

Further along the street, the reporter stops to talk with two young policemen.

First Policeman: "We received a call from Campus Security early this afternoon during a demonstration. When we got there, a couple of hundred kids started pelting us. We broke it up but I guess they decided to hit during the night by wrecking Monument Street."

Second Policeman: "I just saw a few of them actually throwing stuff. A lot of them were just standing there, watching. They were just curious, they weren't trying to hurt us."

Slowly, through careful research and by talking to almost anyone he could find who witnessed some part of the incident, the reporter is able to reconstruct what happened with a fair degree of accuracy through cross-checking each contention.

Naturally, the accounts of the events fell into two general categories: the accounts which favored the viewpoint of student activists, and the accounts which supported the police viewpoint.

After hours of research, the reporter is ready to call in his initial aftermath feature story which emphasizes the "mood piece" approach.

DICTATING STORIES FROM CONFUSED AREAS

Finding a telephone booth that allows the reporter to phone in the story while watching for new flare-ups of violence, the reporter calls in his initial story. As a veteran reporter, he carefully follows the rules of dictating a story:

1. If possible, write out the story first. If it isn't possible to write out the entire story, at least scribble a strong lead on the back of your notepad.

The possible distractions in calling in a story are numerous and troublesome. Only a top professional can skillfully compose a story from raw notes, clearly dictate it, while watching a fresh confrontation develop. Whenever possible, the reporter should at least scribble down a rough version which can be smoothed out by a rewrite man.

2. Be calm and detached. Don't become excited while talking into a telephone.

This often requires a great deal of self-discipline. Once, a radio newsman was sent to cover an industrial accident in which several people were killed. His "live" news accounts were so filled with emotion that the story was lost somewhere in the long string of hyperbolic adjectives.

3. Speak slowly and distinctly.

When your adrenalin is surging, it is difficult to remember that the newsman on the other end of the telephone line cannot possibly type as fast as you can talk, nor can he understand the prattle of hysteria.

4. Read the story—or dictate it from raw notes—one phrase at a time and adjust to the rewrite man's typing speed.

A good rewrite man will lift the pressure bar from his typewriter carriage so that the reporter who is dictating the story can easily hear the clatter of a hurrying typewriter, or the silence that occurs when the rewrite man has caught up. Two veterans working together may complete such dictation with no more than a half dozen time-consuming words spoken between them, other than the dictation.

5. Spell out names and difficult-to-understand words.

Many reporters will spell out any proper name, unless it is so familiar that there can be no misunderstanding. While a reporter may not spell out F-O-R-D when referring to President Gerald Ford, he may carefully, phonetically, spell out a diplomat's name.

If, even in the context of the sentence, a word may be misunderstood or misspelled, then the reporter may spell out the word.

6. If the story information needs to be doublechecked, or if additional calls or research is needed, the reporter should carefully emphasize this to the rewrite man. On most newspapers, the rewrite man inherits the job of such leg work when the reporter is in a remote area or otherwise physically unable to provide his own detailed research.

Often, the reporter will even apprise the rewrite man of "hunches" or sidebar ideas so that, time permitting, his newspaper will have the best possible edge over competition.

EXERCISES

1. Clip a major disaster story from your newspaper. Devise a plan for aftermath story coverage. Who would you interview? How would you approach people to convince them to talk with you? What special problems would you probably encounter in such an assignment? How would you plan to avert the problem?

2. Using information from the campus riot story that is used as an example in Chapter 15, write an aftermath feature story that emphasizes mood piece approach. How can you establish a point of identification for readers? What emotions can you appeal to?

15   Enterprise Stories

In an academic atmosphere, teachers often tend to categorize or classify arbitrarily. Lines are drawn to carefully separate closely similar forms so that students may more easily comprehend characteristics of each form. Journalism teachers often emphasize the sharp, clear line between news stories and feature stories, so that students may understand writing and reporting peculiarities of each.

The problem is that such a separation, while perhaps necessary academically, is artificial and inadequate. Professional journalists cross the line repeatedly, without qualms.

Perhaps a hard news story, particularly a "second day" or follow-up story, may be written in feature style, even while meeting all necessary criteria for a strong hard news story.

Perhaps a feature story evolves into a major informational piece in which new disclosures about a subject may carry great impact on the public.

"Now, we don't even use the term feature story. We refer to just about anything which isn't hard news as being an enterprise piece," a respected editor told a feature writing class.

The first impulse of the teacher was to cringe. After all, the editor had said, in effect, that he was teaching a subject that is as practical as advanced dinosaur tracking. After considering the remark for a moment, the teacher then realized that the editor was purposely overstating the point in order to bridge the artificial gap between hard news and feature writing. Feature writing and hard news writing are different manifestations of the same substance: journalistic writing.

Picture a pencil. The pencil has an eraser and a point, and each extremity has a different function. Yet they are both part of the pencil —part of the same entity.

No clear point of separation exists between hard news writing and feature writing. Instead, a great overlapping area exists between these extremities which may be called "Enterprise Writing."

By definition, an enterprise piece is an analysis or elaboration of a significant situation that affects or potentially affects your readers.

The definition allows great latitude, as you can see. Inflation, for example, isn't an event, it is a situation that affects every reader. A simple news story announcing a higher rate of inflation during the past six months can easily become an enterprise piece by carefully analyzing the causes and effects of that inflation; or it can become a feature story on one family's desperate struggle to pay bills in an inflated economy.

In all three stories, the message may be essentially the same. The difference is in the manner in which that message is presented.

In the discussion of various types of enterprise stories which will follow, sound arguments may be made that the stories are actually news or feature stories. The point is irrelevant. Instead, the real point is this: a writer must never allow rules or format to shackle his ability to communicate. The lesson of the enterprise story is that the writer is obliged to use his initiative, imagination and writing talents to serve the reader by informing him. That, rather than any obligation to strict writing forms, is the writer's sole job.

TYPES OF ENTERPRISE PIECES

While examples and types of enterprise pieces are unlimited, the following are among the more common types:

Controversies

The reporter researches *all* sides of a controversy, the claims and counter-claims, and the nature of the people involved so that readers may study a balanced and complete account of the situation and, in so doing, arrive at their own conclusions.

Perhaps black and white police officers in your city are angry at one another. Black officers claim that promotional exams are culturally weighted to favor white officers, and that white commanding officers carefully groom white officers for civil service tests.

White officers may claim that the black officers are trying to have the test weighted to favor them, at the expense of white officers. Bitterness between the factions grows until it is a serious morale problem that threatens the effectiveness of the police force.

The reporter would interview leaders on each side of the issue, verify or correct charges that are made, and carefully write a sensitive story that succeeds in explaining the problem from each point of view without drawing conclusions.

Situation Pieces

The reporter may bring a significant situation to the attention of the reader which would otherwise escape his notice. The situation piece would also explore the consequences and implications of the situation so that readers may be aware of how the situation might affect them.

Perhaps the sale of cocaine in your community has become a major problem. Heroin addicts, who received treatment at Methadone Treatment Centers, have turned to cocaine for the thrill of drug use. Cocaine has spread into secondary, and even primary, schools and the human tragedy of drug use is growing alarmingly.

The reporter may write an enterprise story on cocaine use after interviewing psychologists, chemists, policemen, heroin and cocaine users, students and almost anyone else who can offer insight to the problem. The result would be an article that gives the public accurate information defining the problem and the alternatives available to each person and to the public as a whole.

News Background

The reporter may write a news background story to explain to readers how a major event occurred, and various implications and alternatives which the public must now face.

Perhaps two local street gangs have been involved in a bloody series of street fights which has caused several deaths. The reporter may spend days talking to the members of each gang to explain, to readers, what the violence is all about.

The Insight Story

Normally written about political subjects, the insight story allows the reporter to reveal the background and subtle, yet significant, information that he gleans from his many political sources and to explain to readers the inner workings of politics, as well as the intricacies of current political intrigue.

If a major political power struggle is taking place behind the scenes in city hall, then the readers are certainly entitled to know about the maneuverings of elected officials and public servants. The city hall reporter may use well-protected, anonymous sources to inform the public so that the public may exert its collective will on the officials.

A variation is the standard election coverage in which the reporter discusses the possible outcome with knowledgeable politicians to provide readers with an accurate prognostication of the results and the factors on which the results may depend.

An astute politician may often predict the results of future elections by fractions of a percentage point. Such stories not only appeal to the reader's curiosity, but do much to contribute to the growing political sophistication of the average American voter.

RESEARCHING THE ENTERPRISE STORY

The research for an enterprise piece is essentially an exercise in good, basic reporting.:

1. Do not pass over a single, possible source of information. Interview everyone who has—or may have—a viewpoint, expertise or knowledge of a situation.

Reporters, as human beings, occasionally become lazy, too. The temptation to summarily dismiss a low-potential news source as being "unnecessary" has cost many reporters key information for their stories.

Once, an investigative team of reporters sought information about major gambling rings in their city. One reporter, who was researching "numbers gambling," knew about a bar that specialized in this lottery-style vice. Yet, the bar was an extremely rough establishment, and the chances of getting someone to discuss the gambling with reporters was considered remote. Although this reporter passed up the "lead," a colleague on the team didn't. After spending hours talking with customers and the bartender, the reporter emerged with a wealth of vital information.

2. Always check clippings in the reference library (newspaper morgue) and other written sources for background information. A great deal of time can often be saved by the simple routine of checking past stories for information and story leads that have already been established.

3. Carefully check out each prevalent rumor that concerns the subject and include the rumor, along with the results of your efforts to verify or dismiss it, in the story. Whether a rumor is valid or not is of only passing interest. The real key is whether people believe the rumor.

4. If unfavorable accusations or material is uncovered, confront the person who is accused and give him ample opportunity to clarify or rebut. While circumstances may appear to implicate the individual

beyond a reasonable doubt, strange coincidences and accidents may add up to a bizarre, but innocent chain of events.

A prime rule of journalism is to always seek the "other side" in any argument or controversy. This rule has kept more than one reporter out of court in libel cases.

5. Look for a focal point: an individual case to illustrate the main thrust of the story. A human example is much easier to comprehend than a complicated, through accurate, abstract explanation.

A story about inflation may contain weighty advice and explanations from economists which would be unpalatable for most readers. Yet, taking the same information, the writer can make it readable and even attractive by using a real family of four people to illustrate, through example, how the inflation process works.

The Process of Research

By logically organizing his efforts, the reporter can effectively and efficiently explore all relevant aspects of his story subject in the time he may allot to the project.

1. At the outset, make a list of what information you have already available, and what information must be gathered. This initial "shoping list" will, inevitably, be expanded or deleted as the reporter becomes more aware of the specific nature of his story subject. Yet, from the first, the reporter is forced to carefully organize his efforts and avoid time-wasting duplication or thoughtless actions which rarely pay off.

2. List all possible sources of information that you must yet gather. List these informational sources in order of expected productivity. As soon as the information is uncovered and verified, the reporter may discard low-rated sources.

3. As soon as the story begins to take shape, make a rough outline of the story, as it appears at that moment. While the outline is a valuable guideline, reporters must be careful not to allow that outline to dictate the nature of the story, sometimes distorting it. If new information tends to undermine your story outline, throw out the outline, not the new information.

4. Toward the end of your investigation, write a rough draft to spot informational holes. In writing a long story, the initial rough draft will almost invariably turn up major holes that will send the reporter scurrying back to sources for important information.

5. After preliminary research, make a new list of information that you have on hand, and information that you need to gather for the story.

Writing an Enterprise Story

The problem of achieving objectivity and a fair, comprehensive presentation of material necessitates the establishment of two general rules before the first word is written:

Do not draw conclusions, just render the facts that you have gathered and let the readers determine the ultimate truth.

Never try to "slant" a story so that it leads to a conclusion. While subtler than simply stating conclusions, the act of purposefully slanting a story reduces the story to the level of malign propaganda.

To elaborate on these rules, if a reporter succeeds in fully researching the material and presenting all relevant information, then the reader should have no trouble making up his own mind, because the facts will speak for themselves.

The act of slanting or drawing a conclusion is, in fact, an open admission of failure by the reporter. Since he is either unable to sufficiently research the material to establish the truth, or is unable to communicate effectively the material he has found, he is resorting either to asking the reader to "take my word for it" in drawing conclusions, or to playing cheap "word tricks" through slanting.

Besides the obvious ethical considerations—slanting and drawing conclusions are not ethical techniques—these two evils also greatly enhance the chance of libel action. The victim of the article may rightly claim that he was injustly and deliberately maligned by unproven allegations.

To summarize, the reporter should always remember that a remote possibility exists that he is drawing the wrong conclusion, and the impact of his error could be substantial when 200,000 or so people are exposed to it.

Besides these two general rules, several writing tips are available to help the reporter in writing enterprise stories:

1. An enterprise story must generally follow the inverted pyramid. Because of its close kinship to hard news stories, the enterprise story normally requires rigid adherence to the traditional organization.

Perhaps the traditional inverted pyramid may be altered into the modified form of the inverted "Christmas tree," in which each viewpoint or informational segment is presented as a complete increment. In this structure, the last item in one segment of information may be much less interesting or important than the first item in the following segment. The arrangement is that of *blocks* of material, not individual items. The inverted "Christmas tree" is illustrated below:

THE INVERTED CHRISTMAS TREE

Lead

Bridge

Segment 1

Segment 2

Segment 3 (etc.)

2. Anecdotes are vital. Use them as you did in the lengthy personal profile Story (Chapter 12): as gems to sprinkle throughout to keep readers interested.

In the use of anecdotes, the enterprise story borrows one of the best techniques from the feature writing side of its heritage. The anecdotes are especially necessary when dealing with complex, essentially dull material of great significance to the reader. The example of the use of a real family to illustrate the effects of inflation illustrates this need well.

3. Terse, effective writing is a vital quality. While the need for such succinct writing has been emphasized repeatedly in other chapters, it is well to remember that the need for brevity *increases* with the length of the story, because the reader may quickly stop reading if the story bogs down.

4. Every assertion made in the story must be well proven with documentation that is solid enough to withstand courtroom questioning. If the story is the least bit damaging to someone's position or reputation, he may have no recourse but to file a libel suit against your newspaper, even if he is actually guilty of wrongdoing.

Almost any aggressive reporter will, some day, face the threat of libel action, for either real or imagined offense. Very few libel actions actually result in courtroom victories or significant out-of-court settlements for the plaintiff. Yet the reporter must be aware that such a loss would severely damage his career and his reputation, even if he is correct in his accusations. *Accusations must be provable.*

To avoid the embarrassment of libel action, many reporters follow this system:

Ask yourself: Can I prove it in court? If the answer is no, the reporter must either delete that charge from the story or work harder to find proof of the allegation.

Is there any conceivable explanation for that person's apparently illegal, unethical or immoral behavior that is the basis of the allegation? The reporter should confront the subject and allow him the rebut or explain. This is an effective defense against libel because, if the person is innocent of wrongdoing, he can establish his innocence with the reporter. If he is guilty, then he may give extenuating circumstances. And if he is innocent, but he refuses to talk with the reporter about the charge, the newspaper's lawyers may have the case dismissed on the grounds that the reporter took every prudent step to ascertain the truth and the plaintiff had only himself to blame for not clearing up the misconception.

Carefully assess the story for passages which may have double-meaning, or that may be misinterpreted. Libel may result from professional negligence, as well as commission.

APPLICATION OF ENTERPRISE REPORTING

Stories that fall into this overlapping area between feature writing and hard news writing are vital tools in the coverage of complex institutions such as on the city hall beat. No other news beat can even approach that for its preponderance of subtle, complex situations that have great opportunities for affecting many readers.

When he isn't writing light features or sorting through complicated public meetings for hard news, the city hall reporter spends a great deal of time checking the human barometers that faithfully gauge the subtle shifts of bureaucratic power and political intrigue.

Some reporters even establish a routine checking procedure designed to discourage officials from yielding to temptation to abuse their power or misuse public funds.

One reporter routinely checked city hall expense accounts, which are public record. Friendly and honest officials secretly loaned their expertise to help the reporter spot irregularities in payments for out-of-town travel expenses. The enterprise stories that resulted from the expense account checks served to boost public esteem for officials who were thrifty with public funds, and created pressure on those who abused their expense accounts by "living it up" on public monies. While a relatively small amount of money was involved in such expense accounts, the reporter was pleased when city hall sources told him that the articles had made officials much more conscious of their public obligation, and that they reminded less ethical officials that the press was, indeed, serving the function of an aggressive watchdog of public interest.

On police beat, the reporter must be constantly alert for any indication of corruption or abuse of authority—two all-too-common evils which may destroy the morale of a police department and its public support. Honest officers will frequently tip reporters to corruption or abuses so that the undesirable members of the police force may be weeded out.

The courts beat reporter may closely watch for patterns of chicanery. Perhaps a municipal court judge's former law partner regularly achieves an inordinate number of acquittals in the judge's court. Perhaps a judge has displayed poor judgment in granting probation for offenders who promptly commit other crimes when released. Or, perhaps another judge has been absurdly strict in meting sentences to relatively minor, first-time drug offenders. While most judges maintain irreproachable reputations for honesty and prudence, the court reporter must be aware that human frailties may occur from even the august loftiness of a judicial bench.

Whatever beat a reporter may inherit, the enterprise story will quickly become a major tool for him. The enterprise story, and all the variations that may be grouped under the heading, offer the reporter the opportunity to rise above the constraints of being merely a good writer, or a good newsgatherer. The enterprise story allows the reporter to assume the role of the investigator or watchdog who guards the public interest by uncovering and clearly defining problems and transgressions that are against public interest.

Critics of journalism sometimes charge that such investigative or interpretative reporting invariably turns journalists into callous cynics who view the world as a cesspool of scandal and corruption where honesty and integrity are rarely found and, in any case, are highly suspect. In fact, the best investigative reporters often publicly declare that corruption and scandal are the exception, rather than the rule, in American governments, and their efforts to purge such corrupt elements is, in fact, a testimonial to the inherent strength of our government.

EXERCISES

1. List five enterprise story topics that can be written about subjects on campus. Explain how each idea is of interest to the public and, generally, how you would research it. Give the list to your instructor and let him select a topic from your list. Write a 4-page enterprise story on the topic selected.

2. Some enterprise story topics are almost universally applicable to college campuses. Students may be divided into teams to research the following topics:

a) Are students being charged a fair rent for off-campus apartments? Do apartments meet city building code specifications? Are damage deposits fairly administered? What is the overall situation related to off-campus rentals?

b) Who runs the student government? Do fraternities and sororities exercise undue influence over student elections? Do students tend to be apathetic? Is there an "in" group that normally determines student government offices?

c) Are student fees properly administered? Where does each dollar go? How much say-so does each student have in the spending of his money?

d) What is the campus crime situation? Do campus police investigate felonies, or are city police called in? Is security on campus adequate to protect students from crime? What kinds of offenses are most common?

16 : Writing a Series

Frequently, the work of enterprise story research turns up so much material that a single story is impractical. The editors decide that so much information is available that, to do justice to the story, it must be presented in the form of installments.

The decision on whether to run the material in series form or as a major Sunday, full-page spread is often difficult, with the editors mulling over these factors:

Advantages of a Series

1. Each day's installment is short enough that it does not discourage the reader from undertaking the article. The full-page spread requires a great commitment of time from the reader. Few people are normally willing to invest that time in a single article.

2. Each installment receives better play than the full-page spread, which is normally relegated to an inside page with, perhaps, a page-one promotional plug. A good series may demand page-one play each day it runs.

3. A series is normally better-promoted than the single, full-page spread. Because the series requires a greater commitment from the editors, the promotional efforts to gain maximum effect from a series are often considerable.

4. The work simply gains more mileage for the reporter than the full-page spread. An editor can hardly fail to notice and appreciate the efforts of a reporter whose series dominates page one for a week.

From the editor's viewpoint, the series provides an excellent way of rewarding a good reporter for his effort.

Disadvantages of a Series

1. If a reader misses one installment, he may be inclined to disregard the remaining installments on the often-erroneous notion that, by missing one story, he will be unable to understand subsequent ones. If that missing installment is one of the early ones, a great deal of the reporter's work will then have gone for naught.

2. A series entails much redundancy. To avoid losing readers in the situation described above, most reporters insert considerable background high in each installment of the series so that the reader can easily understand it. Names, terms and situations must, in any case, be well defined or identified in each separate installment whereas, in a single, full-page spread, repeated definitions and identifications would be unnecessary.

3. It is difficult for a reporter to make each installment of the same high quality that characterized the others. Almost every lengthy series has at least one weak link which can lose many readers who may become bored with that segment.

4. A series requires a major commitment from the editors. After seeing only the first couple of installments, the editors are asked to commit themselves to many column inches of space, and to place the reputation of the newspaper on the line in promoting a series which hasn't been completely written.

A reporter may only have the rough draft when the editors make their decision. That decision may be based on the reporter's summary of what information he has uncovered, the writing that is exhibited in that rough draft, and the reporter's reputation. Frequently, a series may begin with the last few installments still in the reporter's mind and notebook. If the newspaper advertises a seven-part series, it must print seven installments, even if the last four parts are substandard.

RESEARCHING A SERIES

The first step in any journalistic project is to decide, specifically, on the nature of the story you will write. If a series is to be written, then the writer must undertake a subject that is sufficiently broad to provide ample, interesting material for several installments.

Realistically, few series start out *as series*. A reporter may be intrigued by conditions in the city jail and by an inordinate number of suicides there. He may begin his investigation with the concept of a single, in-depth story. Yet, the more he probes, the more interesting material is uncovered so that, ultimately, the scope of the story is simply too broad for a single story. The alternative is a series.

Another series may evolve from a vague directive to "find out what you can about street gangs" which a reporter may receive from his city editor. The reporter would begin his research without even a hint of the ultimate use of his fact-finding and, three weeks later, he may find himself struggling with a six-part series on street gangs.

Some series are carefully planned before the reporter researches the first fact. An enterprise-styled series may begin with a vague concept in the mind of the managing editor. The concept may be based on the rising rate of reported crime in the city, and various indications that citizens are living in fear of crime. Calling a veteran police reporter into his office, the managing editor may say:

"I want you to write a series that will put crime in a proper perspective. I want to know who commits crime, who are the victims, how efficient is the police department, how I can avoid becoming a victim, the profits of crime, and anything else that would help me to understand the real nature of the threat."

We shall return to the crime series shortly, but let's examine a few other types of series first.

Such non-newsworthy situations as tips for filling out income tax forms, home improvement projects, gardening tips, or ecology advice can easily provide series topics. Some newspapers carry such columns regularly. For example, consumer advocate reporter may write a brief column on consumer advice each day.

Special people may provide ample material for series. In almost any election, the reporter who covers a major campaign may write a series of personality sketches or even full-length personal profiles on the candidates. Each candidate, regardless of his chances of winning, would receive equal coverage. Such a series would provide invaluable information to voters.

Other "people" series may include such topics as the city's most prominent businessmen and women, top city officials, ministers, artists, people with unusual jobs or other common bonds. A "people" series may also focus public attention on a serious problem—such as about inmates in a mental institution, or about elderly people in nursing homes.

Still another general type is the news series, designed to give special background or insight to a situation or event that is current. The public may or may not be aware of that situation or event, and the series may be weighted toward straight, hard-news style if the information uncovered is of major consequence.

More often, the news series simply penetrates far beneath the famous who-what-when-where of newswriting, and focuses on the most difficult "w"—Why?

The crime series, mentioned earlier, is one example of the news series. Other news series may examine the structure, operation and impact of local gambling, an analysis of the city's economy, an in-depth analysis of political patronage and corruption, and the local ties to national organized crime.

Some series topics may, in effect, fall in-between the news series and non-news series. A series that examines the "slum lord" system in which absentee landlords, often wealthy investors, allow ghetto housing to degenerate into conditions that violate health and safety standards. By explaining the situation and naming the "slum lords," a newspaper can force such owners to at least adhere to city health and safety code standards through forming a strong, negative public reaction against them.

"It really hurts your standing at the country club if you are exposed as a slum lord," a reporter, who had written such a series, once said.

The *Miami Herald,* alarmed at the increasing numbers of retired —or semi-retired—mobsters who were moving into the area, once ran a series entitled "Know Your Neighbors." The series featured a photograph of a home and information identifying the owner's criminal record, and mob connections. Many Miami residents were shocked when they discovered that the "nice guy next door" was a major figure in organized crime.

Regardless of the origin of the series idea, or the specific subject of the series, the job of researching and writing the series is a major undertaking. It will require careful planning and often painfully tedious research.

A RESEARCH EXAMPLE

Let's return to the crime series. After receiving his general instructions from the managing editor, the reporter ponders the concept and begins to jot down some rough thoughts which must be clarified before planning can begin.

Here are some of the more obvious questions:

1. From which basic viewpoint should the series be written? Among the many possibilities are: the victim's viewpoint, the criminal's viewpoint, the police viewpoint, the insurance company viewpoint, or all of the above.

2. How much time will the reporter be given for research? The series is obviously a major undertaking, but to

release a reporter from other duties for several months is a commitment of several thousand dollars on the part of the newspaper.

3. What are the general boundaries of the series? Should related areas, such as insurance costs, traffic offenses, real estate costs in high-crime areas compared to low-crime areas, and the effects of crime-related injuries and disability on sick-leave at industrial plants be considered?

4. How much money is the newspaper willing to invest in related expenses, such as travel to other cities to compare law enforcement approaches and crime problems, or for undercover work in bars where criminals may frequent? Or money to pay informants?

A second meeting is held in the managing editor's office, at which the city editor, assistant managing editor and assistant city editor also attend. After a prolonged discussion, these and other questions are settled so that the reporter knows precisely what resources he has available and, more specifically, what his focus must be.

In this case, the managing editor may tell the reporter that he is assigned to this project full-time, with minimal extra responsibilities until the project is completed. He may take several months, if necessary, to complete the project. He is to remain in the city, and restrict his research to city sources.

After the meeting, the reporter is ready to specifically outline the information he will need to gather, and the sources of information which must be contacted. Such a list may run a dozen pages, and include contacts with the police chief, the police lieutenant in charge of detectives, the commander of the organized crime control squad, sergeants who head such squads as vice, robbery, homicide, burglary, larceny, fraud, and other functions. Key uniformed officers would also be contacted, particularly those who patrol rough neighborhoods, or who have solid reputations as top-rated veterans. The police psychologist, the top training officers, the historian, the officer in charge of data collection, and many other prime police sources would be interviewed.

Then, the victims would be sought out. The reporter may plan to spend several hours riding with uniformed officers to interview victims of crimes. He may call victims, whose names are listed on police offense reports, to get their side of the story. He may talk to psychologists who have treated crime victims who suffered from mental problems as a result. Physicians who treat victims in emergency wards may provide insight.

Interviewing the criminals may be the most difficult job. Using police contacts, however, arrangements may be made to talk with minor criminals who often double as police informants. Prostitutes, drug pushers, bookies, and even some burglars and muggers can be reached through police. To supplement this limited information, police computerized information can be used to draw statistical profiles of the criminals. Court probation officers may also add great insight.

Beyond the three most obvious viewpoints—police, criminals and victims—several tangent viewpoints are available. Judges may explain the critical problems of an overloaded docket, and the dilemma of choosing between a prison sentence to an institution that provides no rehabilitation or releasing the convict on probation, knowing that he may very well commit another crime.

Prisons are still another related area. Does rehabilitation exist at prisons? Do prisoners return to society with an even more vicious nature after several years incarceration? What can be done to improve the prison system?

Sometimes, research will lead a reporter into a mind-boggling flood of information which is almost beyond his ability to comprehend, much less explain to his readers.

Perhaps the reporter is trying to determine the cost of crime to society. On first glance, it may seem easy: simply ask for the total property value reported stolen, according to the police computer. Then the reporter discovers that this is inadequate, because it does not really approximate the total value of all stolen property, since many—perhaps most—crimes are not reported to police. While the police may have $2 million in total reported losses to crime, a burglary detective may laugh at the figure.

"The narcotics detectives estimate that we have 500 heroin addicts in town, with an average habit of $50 a day," the detective says. "This $50-a-day habit is above and beyond the amount of money he needs for food, clothing and housing. His habit doesn't take weekends off, so he needs $350 a week. This figures out roughly to about $9 million a year that's spent for drugs. Where do you think most of that money comes from, the Good Fairy? They steal it or sell themselves for it.

"Now, let's say that they steal property through a burglary. How much do you suppose a burglar gets for a $100 television set? He gets $20 from the 'fence' who sells it to the nice, honest citizen for $75. The honest citizen is greedy enough to buy 'hot' goods, but too chicken to steal them himself. So, if a burglar must steal enough to buy $50-a-day worth of drugs, the goods must be worth $250. If even half of our addicts support their habits through burglary, the $2 million loss figure is absurd. And don't forget that addicts are only a fraction of our burglars."

Leaving police headquarters after the talk with the detective, the reporter may be depressed at the implication of the discussion. Crime is much, much worse than the public thinks because people are simply not complaining to police.

After returning to the newsroom, the reporter may chat with the labor beat reporter about his project. When the reporter outlined his findings on the cost of crime, the labor beat reporter could have a rude shock in store for him.

"That's only the tip of the iceberg," the labor reporter says. "What about the costs in sickleave? What about medication and hospitalization costs for victims? Or funeral costs? For that matter, what about the intangible costs in human suffering? I know a bricklayer whose wife was beaten by a mugger two years ago. She is a psychological basket-case. She wakes up in the middle of the night screaming. She is afraid to be alone, even for a moment."

Later, in a conversation with the detective sergeant in charge of larceny, the reporter receives still another jolt:

"What about victimless crimes?" the sergeant asked. "Prostitution, gambling and narcotics are all illegal, but these illegal transactions are never reported. Take gambling, for instance. I know men who bet their whole paychecks on horseraces through bookies each week. Their families don't eat if they lose. The families are the victims.

"Also, what about shoplifting and so-called white-collar crimes? Do you know that most stores jack up the prices on all items by three or four per cent to cover shoplifhting and employee theft losses? You wouldn't believe it if I told you who the shoplifters are. As often as not, they are respectable, middle-class housewives or husbands who risk their whole reputations to steal a $2 pair of socks. As for employee theft, seemingly honest people often convince themselves that they are underpaid, so it really isn't stealing to take a few tools and products home."

The frustrated reporter may decide that, at last, he is apprised of the problem of deriving a figure for the cost of crime. Then, in a conversation with his city editor, another facet is unveiled:

"What about the associated costs of crime, such as the cost of law enforcement, incarceration, the judicial system, and the prison system? When you think about it, there's a whole army of policemen, judges, clerks, guards, federal agents, and even businesses such as burglary alarm systems and weapons, that depend on crime for their livelihood. How are you going to come up with a figure on these costs?" the city editor says.

To keep this example in perspective, remember that the cost of crime is only one aspect of the series subject, as a whole. Obviously, the reporter could spend months researching this single aspect without ever achieving a realistic estimate. Yet, the reporter must perform enough research to at least establish the major points within the framework of crime costs.

In the formal research, each contact is well-planned. Before interviewing the homicide sergeant, the reporter may list several dozen key questions which must be answered, such as:

1. How many homicides occurred last year within the city?

2. What is the statistical breakdown, according to the nature of the weapon used?

3. How many of these crimes are solved?

4. What is the relationship between victims and assailants?

5. What circumstances most often lead to homicides?

6. Are homicides more common in certain areas? Which areas?

7. Are cheap handguns, called "Saturday Night Specials," a significant factor in the rising rate of homicides?

8. Is first degree murder common?

9. How can you lessen the likelihood of becoming a murder victim?

These and other questions would be designed to carefully lead the sergeant through a deep discussion of his area of expertise. But the reporter must always be prepared to set aside his questions when an unexpected, interesting area is opened.

For example, when the reporter added the fourth question, concerning the relationship between victims and assailants, he was specifically interested to find out whether strangers were often murderers, or whether family and friends were more likely culprits. While answering the question, the sergeant may say:

"It's kind of interesting how violence begets violence. People who hang around rough areas may be witnesses on one murder, suspects on another, or victims of still another."

The reporter quickly pursued this fascinating opening: "Can you think of examples?"

"Yeah, remember Charlie Evans?" the sergeant said. "Evans was a witness to the murder of Mildred Sands in the Owlhead Bar last May. In June, he was arrested for the murder of Arnold Jones. In December, the night before he was supposed to be tried for that murder, Evans was killed during a fight at the Owlhead."

Such anecdotes are always valuable, so the reporter questioned the sergeant at length to gather other specific examples of violent crimes which would help readers to better understand the nature of the crimes. As an expert, the sergeant's own viewpoint is of legitimate value to the story. If, for example, the sergeant should favor banning handguns, it can be a significant point in the installment on homicides.

Each interview with each possible source of information in the formal research stage is a major undertaking which may exhaust both the reporter and the source. Interviews with victims and criminals may be nerve-wracking and unpleasant, but, slowly, the story begins to take shape in the available information.

When the initial research stage is completed, the reporter may make a new outline that will serve to make him aware of missing data. The outline is not a serious attempt to structure the ultimate series. Instead, it serves as a checklist, and a means by which the reporter may assess the direction his research is leading.

SECONDARY RESEARCH

In the secondary research stage, the reporter returns to initial sources to gain information missed during the first interview, performs tedious documentary research, and makes initial contacts with additional sources who have been identified in the primary research stage.

Perhaps, in the interview with the burglary sergeant, the reporter forgot to ask for tips on protecting your home from burglars. A second interview would be needed to complete the research in that area.

The documentary research is time-consuming and unglamorous. Written material concerning crime is too abundant for a comprehensive compilation, but major written sources that would be needed include:

The Federal Bureau of Investigation's Uniform Crime Reports for several years. These official records of major crimes in the U.S. and in cities, towns and villages, would provide valuable comparative data. The reporter's own city would also be listed, and the number of crimes in each classification would be given for each year. With a careful study, the reporter could statistically analyze reported crime to show readers any patterns that may emerge.

Police manpower statistics. The F.B.I. Uniform Crime Reports provide a listing that shows the number of police officers in each city, the city's population, and the ratio of officers to citizens. This can indicate whether the city's police force is adequately manned.

The computerized listing of each crime committed in the city during the previous year, the time, date, place where it was committed, the property loss or injury, weapon used, and other relevant material may be obtained through the police public relations office, or through contacts within the data processing operation.

Computer summaries showing composite profiles of the average victim and the average criminal in each crime category.

Reference books on the structure of organized crime, police laboratory technology, sociological studies of crime, and other studies made by reputable authorities.

In such research, a reporter may spend several days, poring over statistics and comparing them, or compiling different statistics from raw data. He must accurately and effectively apply the statistics to his task of painting a realistic, accurate picture of crime. A single mathematical error, or erroneous conclusion seriously damages his credibility and, in turn, negate much of his work.

The third aspect of secondary research—contacting additional informational sources identified during primary research—may be a dangerous stage. Because this is among the last steps in research, the wrapping-up of loose ends, the reporter can easily become tired and careless. After spending two weeks wrestling with statistical data, the reporter may be quite bored with the subject or, possibly, so overloaded with it that he needs a year-long vacation in the West Indies to recuperate. Because of this mental fatigue, the threat of errors becomes much greater. Most veteran reporters become extra-cautious at this stage.

At this point, the research is almost completed. The reporter has contacted everyone who may provide meaningful information, and interviewed each source at length. He has carefully studied every key statistical or documentary source. He had filled several notebooks and folders with raw notes. He is now ready to write.

Writing A Series

Before outlining the series, the reporter and the editors must first decide how many installments would be appropriate.

If the newspaper decides on too many installments, it greatly increases the commitment to the series and also increases the chance that a reader will become bored, or that he will miss an installment and stop reading it. If the series has too few installments, each installment will be far too long, so that the reader will only skim the first few paragraphs of each day's entry.

Many editors contend that the six- or seven-part series is ideal. Such a series would normally start on Sunday and continue through Friday or Sunday, skipping the weak Saturday issue. The logic goes this way:

Sunday is the heaviest circulation day. Many people read only the Sunday newspaper so, by starting a strong series in the Sunday newspaper, you may lure them into subscribing regularly to get the rest of the series. Saturday is, traditionally, a weak issue because many people spend Saturday away from home. Therefore, the series would either end before Saturday or skip that day. On the negative side, some weekday readers do not receive the Sunday newspaper, so after missing the first installment, they may decide not to read the series.

Deciding On Installment Subjects

In the crime series, we shall assume that the editors agree on a six-part series. The reporter must then decide on the most logical groupings so that he may make each installment strong and readable.

The alternatives are myriad. The reporter may write each installment about a certain crime category—such as violent crimes, victimless crimes, robberies, burglaries, thefts, and frauds. Perhaps he could decide to do it by viewpoints: the criminal, the victim, the policeman, the merchant, the insurance company, the judge.

After struggling with the problem, the reporter finally decides on this grouping for the six parts:

1. *The overall impact of crime on the city.* This initial installment would offer a birds-eye view of the problem and its many ramifications.

2. *The criminals.* Who are the criminals? Why did they become criminals? How do they relate to the victims? What does society do with captured criminals? What are the effects of assuming a "life of crime"?

3. *The victims.* Who are the victims? Why did they become victims? What, exactly, did they lose in human as well as material costs? How can you avoid becoming a victim?

4. *Costs of Crime.* As discussed earlier in the chapter, the costs of crime are nebulous and frightening.

5. *Crime Prevention.* What can be done to reduce crime? Can a citizen protect himself against burglaries, robberies, rapes, etc.? What should you do if you are being robbed?

6. *Analysis of the police effectiveness* and the overall prognosis in the "war on crime."

Outlining Each Installment

When the general installment subjects are decided, then the writer must outline each installment so that he knows what is to be included in each. Some material will be overlapping. For example, material related to costs of crime may be appropriate in every installment. Background material must also be inserted in each new installment so that the reader knows essential information that is needed to understand the new installment.

The actual outlining uses essentially the same techniques as those discussed in Chapter 8 on polishing a feature story. In fact, the writing process for each installment is the same as that given in that chapter.

Special Problems of Series Writing

Continuity from one installment to another is the greatest obstacle in series writing.

As discussed earlier, the need to insert background material in each installment after the first is derived from the fact that, in each installment, some material requires information given previously for the reader to adequately understand it.

Let's take the installment on crime prevention. Much of the defense against crime is based on knowing how criminals operate and how victims unknowingly avail themselves to criminals. Thus, in discussing protection, the writer must insert background material that includes information given in the previous two installments.

The decision on how much background material to include may be crucial. An insertion of several paragraphs of background may bore readers who got that information in previous installments, yet, without it, readers who missed the previous installments can't perceive the significance.

THE FINAL DRAFT

Before writing the final draft, the reporter should carefully list the small but important informational gaps and contradictions that became apparent during the earlier writing. Perhaps he finds that a subject's name is spelled differently in two different uses. This is easy to check. In another passage, he may find that two experts seem to be disagreeing about a minor point. He must recontact each expert to make certain that the disagreement really exists. In still another case, he may find that he forgot to ask a source an important question.

After compiling this "shopping list" of minor points, it will be a simple matter for the reporter to quickly ascertain the proper information so that he can write the final draft without interruption.

Guidelines

In preparing a series, the reporter may discover that the task of turning out professional-quality writing on each of the 50 or so double-spaced, 8½ × 11″ pages is a difficult one. In addition to being alert to the minor but sometimes disastrous mistakes that come from mental let-down, the writer must keep these general guidelines in mind:

1. Terseness is vital in series writing. A few sub-standard, verbose paragraphs in one installment may cause some readers to miss the rest of your series.

2. A lengthy diet of facts and statistics will send the reader scrambling to the comics page. Make the facts palatable by providing glittering anecdotes, examples and other entertaining tidbits to enliven your story.

3. Write each installment as a complete story in itself, with only a general reference to other installments. You want to encourage readers who have missed earlier parts to pick up the series.

Sidebars

After spending months of arduous research, a reporter normally gathers interesting material that just doesn't quite fit in any installment, although it may be related. Rather than awkwardly insert the material, thus unduly lengthening the installment, it may be better to write it as a sidebar.

The sidebar offers two advantages: it provides a natural grouping for this material, and it avoids the risk of cluttering the main story. In fact, by writing such material in sidebar fashion, the reporter may enhance its chances of being printed.

If an installment is too long, the copy desk will simply have to chop out some material. The sidebar material, which doesn't really fit naturally into the story, would probably be cut.

In sidebar form, the material may sneak into print because it can compete with other material, on its own merits, for the available space.

Summary

Few other journalistic writing forms can give a reporter the psychological lift of a series. The advance promotion that stimulates the urge to read his series, the ego-trip of front-page position for a week, and the immense satisfaction of achievement that comes with the completion of a major project, may boost a reporter's self-esteem.

Yet, in the heady aftermath of the series, the reporter may overlook a point that is so often true in all areas of journalism: although the reward of recognition is great, the reporter had to pour all of his energy, intelligence and resourcefulness into the effort.

If series writing is a major source of glamour to practicing journalists, then student journalists would be well advised to carefully weigh the costs of that achievement.

A person who becomes a journalist for the recognition alone may soon become disillusioned with the price that must be paid. Yet, a person who enters journalism to make meaningful contributions to society and, perhaps as a secondary objective, to gain recognition, will find that journalism is, indeed, a glamorous profession. If, for example, after all the work and research involved in the crime series, a life was saved or conditions were improved, the reporter who wrote the series could feel great satisfaction.

EXERCISES

1. List five possible series topics available at your school. Explain, in detail, why each of these topics would be of interest to the public. Is there ample material on the subjects to provide a series? Generally, how would you research it?

2. Write a detailed initial outline for a series on the costs of higher education. Decide which viewpoint you will use to achieve focus, and show how you will develop that viewpoint.

Index